# Secure the Blessings of Liberty

## Understanding Our Constitution

Robert K. Jones

Husky Trail Press LLC

Husky Trail Press LLC
PO Box 705
East Lyme, CT 06333
860-739-7644
888-775-5211
860-691-8066 fax
www.huskytrailpress.com

ISBN No. 978-0-9722918-7-3

First edition     10 9 8 7 6 5 4 3 2 1
Printed in the United States of America

To my parents, whose example taught
me that a Life based upon Principle is
a Life without Fear or Panic.

# Contents

## CHAPTER TWELVE

## NOW WHAT

# APPENDICES

## APPENDIX 1

## APPENDIX 2

## APPENDIX 3

## APPENDIX 4

## APPENDIX 5

## APPENDIX 6

# INTRODUCTION

## Why I Wrote This Book and
## Why You Want To Read It!

I have two basic goals in writing this book. I want to convince you of two things:

1. It is possible for you to understand the Constitution for yourself; You don't need "experts" to tell you what it says.
2. It is vitally important that you do so, because the document cannot serve its purpose if you don't.

If I can succeed in those two goals, then more important long-term goals will naturally follow. If you understand its importance and believe you can understand it, you will read it. If large numbers of Americans read the document for themselves, they will not only know if their government exceeds its limits, they will "know that they know." This is not possible without a more universal understanding of the document, and it will naturally flow from a more universal American understanding of it.

In convincing you of these things, I want to avoid actually telling you what is in the document itself. I am going to present information, much of which you already know, and the rest of which is easily obtainable in your local library or over the internet. It is important to understand from the outset that the extraneous material that I will refer to is not the Constitution, and does not supersede or alter it in any way. The Constitution stands alone. However, I need to refer to other documents to prove that it is understandable by the average American.

This may seem like somewhat of a paradox, that I will use outside information to prove that you don't need outside information. However, you need to be prepared for the fact that a lot of those who have positioned themselves as experts will resist this democratization of the Constitution. Such "experts" often refer to these and other materials. You need to at least know these extraneous documents enough to legitimately dismiss their value as evidence proving that you cannot know the secrets of the Constitution.

To begin with, we will need a clear understanding of the nature of the document itself. I will ask you to take a few things on faith for the moment, but I will make those clear, so that if you want to take a highlighter or underline them, and then come back and re-read this section when we get to a certain point in this book, you will be able to see whether or not I proved what I want you to presume for the moment.

**What is the Constitution?** Let's get clear on that much first. The Constitution is the document that creates the federal government. All power and authority of the federal government comes from this document, it cannot expand them at will. Any legitimate action of the federal government will be authorized in this document, and it will moreover tell us what part of the government is charged with the responsibility to do it. That is all that the Constitution does. This will be demonstrated more specifically in the chapter where we look at the document more closely, after we've examined the history leading up to its creation, but for now, take it on faith if necessary the following statement: **"The Constitution creates the Federal government of the United States."**

**What is the purpose of the Constitution?** This question contains some sub-questions and assumptions. Why have a federal government at all? If we are to have a federal government, why limit its power, particularly when voters have so much control over it (assuming you believe that, many do not). We are going to find most of our answers in the Declaration of Independence. For now, take it on faith that **"The purpose for the Constitution is to restrict the government's ability to oppress the People."**

**Does the Constitution have specific meaning?** A lot is

said about the idea that the Constitution is "living, breathing", which is to say that there is no specific and unchanging meaning. I will prove that this is not correct in the sense that is intended by those that put this idea forward, but the two choices are that either the Constitution has a specific meaning or it does not. If that meaning changes over time, then no one can know what it means until it is voted on by those it empowers to decide. That means that it has no meaning at all, beyond empowering those who decide. If it has a specific meaning, then it will even bind those it may empower to decide its meaning to conform to its limits. If it has no meaning, then it could not serve the purpose that we've already assumed (and will later prove), that of limiting the government, and it would have been a pointless effort to write it in the first place. **"The Constitution has a specific meaning."**

Now, if we assume those three things, which will later be demonstrated, one only need apply common sense and logic to see how important it is that you, individually and personally, read and understand the Constitution. The document is intended to protect you, but it can no more do that by its mere existence than a road map can get you to your destination while it remains in your glove compartment – to leave either unread is to trust to Luck or asking others for directions, making it pointless to have either in the first place.

For the Constitution to serve its primary purpose of protecting ordinary citizens from government excess, then the ordinary citizen must be familiar with its contents. I realize that's probably a novel idea, and involves a major paradigm shift for most people. Most people probably don't think they can understand it, for a variety of reasons – none valid. The undeniable fact is that the authors certainly realized that the average person would have to read it for it to serve its purpose. They would have gone out of their way to make it readable for the average person, who in 1786 did not have the ability to search the internet for the answer, they had to be able to understand it on their own. They intended it to be clear, specific, and simple. If they intended it to be vague and mysterious, then the first mystery would be their purpose in putting it on paper and publishing it in the first place.

That's why it is important to you to read the Constitution for yourself. It otherwise cannot protect you from government oppression. It doesn't get any more vital than that.

## WHY WE THINK IT'S DIFFICULT TO READ

Okay, presuming that I've convinced you that you MUST read the Constitution, you may still not be convinced that you are able. One step at a time, just don't use any doubts to justify not giving me the opportunity to persuade you that you are quite capable of understanding it perfectly on your own. All you need is a few tools, and to understand why most people think that it is unknowable to begin with.

We've all read articles regarding "current events" that in one way or another involve the Constitution. There are cases that have been or may in the future be decided in the United States Supreme Court, and there are laws that have been or might be passed in Congress that someone believes might go beyond the Constitution. Even political candidates might be speaking about some plan they have, and some people may wonder whether or not the office they are running for actually carries the power to do whatever it is they intend to do. It might be a local matter, such as a town meeting where someone protests a statue, a seasonal display, or a class in the local schools, claiming that it in some way violates the Constitution.

In reaching our own personal conclusions, we often have no more than what the authors of books or newspaper articles have to say on the subject. We sometimes seem to get conflicting opinions, even among such authors with similar credentials. In the end, we sometimes decide which viewpoint to adopt for ourselves based on what fits with what we already believe to be true, or what our friends and family think, or what we simply want to be true, and if we change our minds at all, it is probably because we find a particular source more credible than another rather than because we read the Constitution for ourselves.

Having been born and raised in this environment where experts differ, the majority of us take it for granted that the Constitution is a very complicated document, and because it was written over two centuries ago, we need experts to tell us what it means. The fact that the experts often disagree only reinforces this belief on our part. Even the fact that many of the more important decisions of the United States Supreme Court are by votes of 5 to 4 reinforces this belief. After all, if at least four of the very people who are charged with the responsibility to know what the Constitution says are clearly wrong, what hope do we have to know without expert advice?

However, there's another way of looking at the exact same information. If the experts are often split on a particular matter, how do we know for certain that the winning side was right? Or is it possible that they are BOTH "right", because the document's meaning really is just a matter of opinion among the Justices of the U.S. Supreme Court?

Yet, there is hope. If you will read this book, forgetting not merely preconceived notions, but much of what you were taught in school and starting with a blank slate, you will be able to know what the Constitution really says, without having to depend on any other source to explain it to you. Let me make it clear that I am not asserting that everything you learned about US History is incorrect. However, if what you know about US History allows you to believe that the Constitution is beyond the capacity of the average person to understand, there is something in your knowledge of the subject that is incomplete. I will present to you the same information that you probably already know, but in a sequence that connects the various events to make it obvious that the Constitution is totally comprehensible.

I realize that the majority of the readers of this book probably believe that trying to read and understand the Constitution is a waste of effort, either because they cannot know what it says, or because they believe there is nothing they can do with the knowledge they gain by reading it. Both beliefs are untrue, and I ask you to temporarily forget what you already learned about it because whatever you learned thus far has led you to those false conclusions. Take what I present in the order presented, and verify any new information there might be independently, and later you can apply what history I do not mention which you already know. What you will find is that I am not presenting a new version of facts, but they are presented in a more logical order, with a few gaps filled in here and there. While I am including copies of most of the documents I will be referring to here for your convenience, I encourage you to compare even those to an alternate source, to ensure I have not altered them in any way.

As I present the information I think is necessary to understand the Constitution, I am going to refer to documents and information besides the document itself. Please do not mistake this for being a contradiction of the following premise:

**The Constitution is a self-contained document.**

For example, I will refer to the Declaration of Independence to illustrate the meaning of parts of the Constitution. Do not take this as an assertion that this or any document whatsoever modifies or alters the Constitution. Other than actual Amendments duly adopted, nothing written after the Constitution changes it, and nothing written before it has any effect on it. I am firm in the belief and will prove that the Constitution is the first and last word on the subject it covers, federal power, but I am forced to deal with the other documents, if for no other reason to counter those who will try to convince you that these other documents do, in fact, have some modifying impact. They are useful tools, but are not authoritative. The Constitution is the "last word."

The first tool you need is a grasp of the nature of the document itself, and the historical context in which it was written. I will go over the general history of the era in which it was written in the next chapter, and you probably won't see much that you do not already know. What might be new is the significance of the facts presented, as the nexus between some of the facts may have been neglected in your fundamental History classes. If you expect a new version of History with some "secret facts", you will be disappointed. What is more likely is that you will read the following chapter and think "Oh! That's why that is important!"

The second tool is that you need to understand is a familiarity with the three major documents that preceded the Constitution. Let me repeat that I'm not saying that they contain any kind of "key" to the "code", it is just that knowing what the Constitution replaced and what situations they were addressing makes it all more readily understandable. It's merely the difference between working out a jigsaw puzzle face-up or face-down. It all fits together the same way in the end, but face-up makes the task a little easier.

The third tool you will need is that you must expect before you read it that it will be something you can understand. Trust me that you will have this expectation before we get to the part where I ask you to actually read it. I realize that if you believed that already, you probably would not be holding this book. You will have the background in History that you will need in order to know what the authors generally intended, and I will suggest a sequence for your first reading that I expect will make the contents leap off the page at you once you read it start to finish, which I ask you not to do now, but will ask you to do so after that sequence.

Finally, you're going to need to have the courage of your own convictions. You are going to embark on a quest for knowledge that most people believe is far beyond your capacity to understand, and many sources attempt to convince you that this is true. You must be prepared to stand by your belief, although there is nothing wrong with discussing differences of opinion with others. You just have to be unwilling to subordinate what you think is true based on your own reading to someone else who is somehow considered an "expert" on the matter.

Let's look at the experts for a moment. What makes a person an "expert" on the Constitution? If you ever talk to one, you'll find that it generally means that the person knows a lot of case law. They have studied what other people have said about the Constitution, particularly the Supreme Court and Appellate Courts. That really doesn't make them experts on the Constitution, it makes them experts on what other people have said about the Constitution. One doesn't become an expert on flowers by reading articles by botanists. Moreover, they are studying some major decisions that were made by a majority of a single vote. If the Supreme Court disagrees on what it says, where does that put the average citizen? For that matter, how can the opinions of anyone not a member of that body, such as lower court judges, attorneys, politicians, reporters, and teachers, have any value at all? The very fact that the body that is regarded as the last word on all matters Constitutional is unable to regularly and uniformly agree may suggest that it isn't worth your effort to know what it says.

**However... that is precisely the reason that it is vital for you to formulate your own opinion first hand. Your only way of knowing is to read it for yourself. You can do it, but if the Supreme Court cannot agree, you must not expect everyone in America to agree with you.**

## WHAT DO I EXPECT YOU TO DO WITH THIS KNOWLEDGE?

We'll go into some specific possibilities later, but generally speaking, what you do with the knowledge is up to you. I have no idea how you will react once you read the Constitution for yourself. If you see a difference between what it says and what you've been led to believe, you may want the Constitution changed to be more like what you've been told it already is, or you may prefer the Constitution as it is to what you've been told, and want the government to follow it and obey its limitations. You may feel one way on some issues, and differently on others. It would contradict the purpose of this book for me to tell you what to think once you've read it for yourself.

The only thing I don't see as being likely is that you conclude that what you've been told about it is accurate. Other than that, I have no specific expectations.

## WHY IT HAS THIS TITLE

The Preamble contains a statement of purpose for the Constitution, which includes the statement "... secure the Blessings of Liberty to ourselves and our Posterity..." It can't do that if the People don't enforce it, and that isn't possible without a widespread knowledge of its contents. I want to promote Liberty by promoting an understanding of the Constitution among the general population, by exploding the myth that it is difficult to understand.

## HOW I CAME TO WRITE THIS BOOK

I spent seven years in the Army. I took an oath on four different occasions which included the promise to "uphold and defend the Constitution of the United States." When I swore that the fourth time, it finally occurred to me that I should read it and see what I was promising. I read it, but to be honest, I couldn't make head nor tail of it.

Years later, when I was in Law School, one of the courses I was required to take was Constitutional Law. Anyone attending Law School in the United States at an ABA-accredited school will have taken this course, and they are probably fairly uniform in structure and content. What I did not realize until some ten years after I had graduated was that while the textbook did contain the full text of the Constitution, it was never required for us to read it in its entirety, and in fact I don't recall it ever actually being suggested or encouraged. Nothing of what preceded the Constitution was ever mentioned at all. For the purposes of the course in Law School, History began with the case that established the United States Supreme Court as the final authority on the Constitution.

The structure of that course was that we would read the decisions of courts, mostly the United States Supreme Court, and analyze them to try to impart to us a uniform understanding of how disputes as to the contents of the Constitution would be resolved in the courts. It apparently never dawned on any of us that we were not studying the Constitution at all, we were analyzing what other people thought about it. The principle of *Stare Decisis*, where courts tended to honor the conclusions of other courts in the past, elevated the words of people writing about the Constitution to have the same status as the Constitution itself, or perhaps greater. This had and continues to have the tendency of making any errors on the subject made by the courts difficult to correct, and even to be compounded over time.

Exacerbating this tendency is the fact that most attorneys tend to be far more familiar with what certain Judges have said and written about the Constitution than with the Constitution itself. It is the nature of the profession that it matters less what the Founders really wrote and meant than it does what the Supreme Court has agreed that they wrote and meant. A lawyer may not care whether or not the phrase "separation of church and state" is in the Constitution as written; if it is in a decision of the U.S. Supreme Court about the Constitution, that makes it one and the same for their purposes. The reverence that should be for the Constitution itself is given to the words of Judges writing about the Constitution.

Adding to the confusion is the fact that the majority of people depend on the media to inform us of what the USSC has said about the Constitution, or an action of the federal government, and we do not even know whether or not the reporters have compared the decision or law to the actual Constitution. We are accepting the opinion of the writer as a fact, when that "fact" is not merely an opinion, it is an opinion about an opinion, when the true facts are knowable by us. We don't have to accept third hand opinions, we could read the Constitution and know for ourselves whether or not anyone had it wrong. If we did that, we'd be equipped to read whatever it might be that is being reported on, and make our own judgment, rather than relying on a report which cannot be independently verified any other way.

So, if you expect this book to contain a lot of case citations, you're going to be disappointed. I'll mention a few cases later on, but only after you're really equipped to look them up for yourself, evaluate them, and decide what's True, rather than simply accept someone else's conclusions.

*Secure the Blessings of Liberty*

# CHAPTER ONE

## A Brief Outline of The History Leading To The Drafting And Ratification of The Constitution Of The United States

There are probably a number of places one can start a discussion of the Constitution itself, once we've ruled out the discussion being one of case law. Even narrowing that down to a historical perspective leaves many options. We could start with the Code of Hammurabi, as the first known written law, or we could start with the Ten Commandments, but the main problem with both is that they are largely sets of laws regarding individual conduct, and not analogous to the Constitution. The Constitution creates a government, which will then be empowered to create laws regarding individual conduct.

We could start with the Magna Carta, and there might be some valid historical reasons for doing so, but the nature of that document is not quite the same as the Constitution; While it did place the Crown under the rule of law in many cases where the monarchy had historically exercised the power to act as it wished, it did not actually create a British government out of nothing, it only limited what the Crown could do in relation to nobles. Furthermore, any action of the Crown not mentioned in the Magna Carta was still permitted, which is the opposite of the Constitution, which prohibits anything not specifically permitted (as we shall also see later).

Given that the Constitution created the government of the United States, it seems that the most logical place to start is in the years before the Revolution; we need to find a point that is within the lifetimes of those who wrote the Constitution, yet before anyone was seriously thinking of Independence.

In 1750, there was no "state" of Massachusetts, nor of

Georgia. They were both colonies of Great Britain, along with everything in between. Politically speaking, this meant that they were subject to the will of the government of Great Britain, both Parliament and the dictates of the King, at least so far as those could be enforced. While the colonists did choose their own local government and write their own laws at times, the King had (or at least "occasionally asserted") the power to nullify those laws, dissolve those governments, and subject the colonies and colonists to laws of his own choosing. They were subject to the laws of Britain, which were more often than not enacted without the participation of colonists in their making, and certainly without the need of gaining their consent. Each colony was the property of Great Britain, and each inhabitant was a subject of the Crown. Generally speaking, this was an acceptable situation to most of the Colonists at that time.

Obviously, some dissatisfaction to this status grew in the following decades, and the causes were largely connected to the imposition of taxes to which the colonies had not consented. The Boston Tea Party of 1773 was a response to a system of import duties intended to specifically favor the East India Company's trade in tea with the colonies, giving them a price advantage over domestic importers who were required to pay a tariff on the same product. It can be argued that the Tea Party was only a protest action, or that it might have been an event in the revolution itself, but that level of detail is unnecessary for our purposes. The important fact that it establishes is that as of 1773, Britain made (and at least attempted to enforce) laws that affected the Colonies, and that some Colonists were already dissatisfied with the results.

The British response to the Tea Party included five Acts which were collectively called by the colonists "the Intolerable Acts." A brief overview follows, and other than their importance to comprehending what followed, the reaction of "who cares?" is understandable, as they have little meaning in and of themselves today. If this were a TV "crime drama", we'd be looking at "motive."

One Act was the closure of the port of Boston in 1774. A blockade was ordered to continue until the East India Company had been compensated for the loss of their property during the Boston Tea Party of 1773, and this effectively punished all Bostonians, most of whom took no part in the raid. Bear in mind that the concepts of "time" and "distance" were different then. With the port of Boston closed, Massachusetts was basically several days over land from the next major port. It took longer to get from Boston to New York then than it takes to get from Boston to Los Angeles today.

Another was an act that clearly made the government of Massachusetts subject to the unilateral will of Britain, all offices to be appointed or replaced from London. Not only were the residents of Massachusetts not represented in London, they were no longer given any voice in their local government, either. This made them powerless to effectively refuse consent to the tariffs to be collected to pay the East India Trading Company for an event in which most of them had no part.

Another allowed trials for acts committed in the colonies to take place in London. This was seen as a mechanism to deny Justice in two different and equally unacceptable ways. One, a colonist whose trial took place in London would be less able to present any witnesses on their own behalf, and would be unable to either pursue a civil claim or defend against a criminal charge in a court several weeks distant from their homes. Two, a government official could commit a serious crime in Boston, and demand to be tried by a jury of people in London, who might be wholly unsympathetic to the victim, an "uncivilized" colonist. Rightly or wrongly, this was the perception of the likely impact of this act.

Probably the least objectionable was the Quartering Act, which allowed the British military forces to use any building for housing troops. Although rarely used to dispossess owners from buildings in current use, the potential alone was considered outrageous. Many of the colonists felt a deep attachment to their landholdings, having cleared the native forest from it and built with their own hands the buildings the Crown asserted the right to peremptorily seize.

The fifth had to do with attempting to influence the Canadian provinces to harass the lower colonies, but that bore little fruit and was more insult than injury.

In response to these Intolerable Acts, the colonies formed the First Continental Congress in 1774, with each of the colonies being invited to send delegates, to determine how best to resist the actions of Britain. At this time, revolution was already being considered by some, but was by no means universal. It is this Congress which adopted the Articles of Association which appears in the first appendix. It is clear from even a cursory reading of the Articles of Association that the desire of that Congress was to reconcile with Britain. Their other major accomplishment was to schedule the meeting of the Second Continental Congress in May of 1775.

In the meantime, the revolution began without the Continental Congress, at Lexington, Massachusetts in April of 1775. It's worth noting in passing that the British objective in that action was to seize the Colonial arsenal, and disarm the colonies, as we'll see their remembrance of that event in the Bill of Rights. It took over a year for the Second Continental Congress to finally conclude that reconciliation with Britain was no longer possible, and it was in the summer of 1776 that they declared their Independence. The Declaration of Independence appears in the second appendix.

As will be shown, this had the effect of making (or at least, "purporting to make") each colony a separate and independent State. As the word "State" is used in the documents here presented, it means an independent sovereign, such that each State was the political equal of Great Britain.

The State of Connecticut, by gaining independence, was as sovereign as the State of France, or the State of Spain. It makes no difference for the purpose of this book whether that became effective when declared, or when Britain ceased to resist that independence and the revolution was over. What is important to realize is that neither the Constitution, nor its predecessor the Articles of Confederation were in existence, so it is clear that no federal government existed as of 1776. Having severed ties with Britain, there were no others, which left each State an independent nation. If that is no longer the case today, we should be able to find some document that makes the change, but very clearly the effect of the colonies' declaring their independence was to cause there to be thirteen new and independent countries on the globe.

Obviously, none of the former colonies were individually prepared to resist any attempt by Britain to use force to quell this insurrection, which Britain continued to attempt to do. Such attempts were more than hypothetical, they were already ongoing. They were fully aware of the need to protect their claimed independence by military force, and that unless they worked together, they would fail separately. Naturally, the most politically influential within each State would be sensitive to trading a subordinate position as part of the British Empire for a subordinate position as part of the American Empire, but they were also sensitive to the fact that the failure of this Revolution would likely mean death by hanging for themselves. They would naturally have been somewhat reluctant to create a system with too much power, but forced to create some kind of union merely to ensure their own survival.

The first document that defined their union was the Articles of Confederation of 1777, appearing in the third Appendix. These Articles will be dealt with in somewhat greater depth in a chapter following, but one important provision to note is Article Two, which specifically reserved the individual

Sovereignty mentioned above. The Articles of Confederation did create the central government of the United States, but the form of the government and its powers were far different from what was to follow in the Constitution.

The Articles of Confederation were replaced by the Constitution in 1787, which appears in Appendix Four, and will be explored in more detail in a later chapter. As said earlier, the Constitution stands alone, and the earlier documents do not alter what it says, but you are going to find it useful to be familiar with them to understand why some provisions are included, and why they chose the structure that they did.

Following the drafting of the Constitution, it still remained for the States to ratify and adopt them. During this period, there appeared a series of newspaper articles written by three members of the authors of the Constitution, John Jay, James Madison, and Alexander Hamilton. It must be stressed that while these are instructive and useful, each of the 85 articles is the work of a single author, and not the actual product that is the Constitution itself. They do not modify the Constitution, they simply are attempts to explain what was written after the fact, and persuade the People to support it. Unlike the Four Great Documents, they are not an act of the government or in the name of the People, they are an explanation of a document. I'll be discussing them after the chapter dealing with the Constitution, but they are not included in their entirety in this book. You can decide whether or not you want to explore them in depth later.

# CHAPTER TWO

## Continuity from The Articles of Association to The Constitution

The Four Great Documents of American History are the Articles of Association, the Declaration of Independence, the Articles of Confederation, and the Constitution. The creation of these spans some twelve years, and are four very different documents in purpose. In fact, the change in sentiment between the drafting of the first two is so drastic, one would almost presume they were written by completely different men.

Yet, this is not entirely true. There were a significant number of the same individuals being involved in multiple documents, as an examination of the roster of signatures of the four shows.

The Articles of Association was signed by thirty-nine men, from nine of the Colonies. Georgia, the Carolinas, and Virginia did not sign onto that document. Of that thirty-nine, fourteen were among the thirty-nine delegates which the colonies returned to sign the Declaration of Independence. When reading the two documents, it bears consideration that fully a quarter of those who signed the Declaration had previously participated in an attempt to resolve the political differences with England peacefully, and as loyal subjects to the Crown.

The Declaration of Independence was signed by fifty-four representatives of the Thirteen Colonies, including the four southern colonies of North and South Carolina, Virginia, and Georgia which abstained from the Articles of Association. Of these fifty-four, fourteen later signed the Articles of Confederation, three of whom had also signed the Articles of Association.

The Articles of Confederation was signed by forty-seven men, and of these, five went on to sign the Constitution. Of these five, two had previously signed the Declaration of Independence, and only one signature, that of Roger Sherman of Connecticut, is found on all four.

In addition, there were three men of the original thirty-nine who also signed the Constitution, but whose signatures are not also found on both of the intervening documents.

What this suggests is that while each of the documents stands alone, and may be fully understood by a reading in isolation, each is a product of the same minds, and probably the same process of thought applied to the same overall goals. The continued participation in the process by a substantial number of the same people evidences the documents as all part of the same process, and that it is possible to gain insight into one through an understanding of any one or all of the other three.

# CHAPTER THREE

## The Articles Of Association
## and
## The Declaration Of Independence

I take these two documents together because, as shown earlier, it was the period in between where the major political shift in the colonies occurred. This shift is most effectively demonstrated by examining them together.

The Articles of Association, shown in Appendix I, clearly shows that the intent of the colonies as of their adoption in 1774 was clearly not to declare independence from Great Britain. It was a compact between the colonies represented by the signers to boycott British goods, particularly those of the East India Company.

The boycott was intended to be a peaceful but hopefully forceful enough protest to persuade Britain to nullify the Intolerable Acts, and it should be noted even gave nearly a year for Britain to decide to do so before the boycott would go into effect. As political demands go, it appears to have been written by men going out of their way to be reasonable, expressing the demand in the most conciliatory of terms.

The opening line "We, his majesty's most loyal subjects" makes it clear that the revolution was not seriously considered at this time. The blame for the grievances of which they complain is laid at the door of "a ruinous system of colony administration, adopted by the British ministry" and "various acts of parliament." At this time, they are apparently appealing to their King for relief, and not blaming him personally for their situation.

Interesting to note is that one of the things included in this boycott was a pledge to "wholly discontinue the slave trade." It goes beyond the scope of this book to fully explore the significance of this provision, but several things are suggested by its presence. One, it indicates that the slave trade was seen by at least some colonists as an undesirable practice, and it is likely that they chose to label it a British trade and practice here as a means to further discourage it in North America. Two, it may explain why the four Southern Colonies (the Carolinas, Virginia, and Georgia) were represented at the drafting of this document, but none of their representatives actually signed it. Three, its presence coupled with the absence of those Southern signatures may actually have foreshadowed the Civil War that was to come upon their grandchildren. While interesting, all of these are entirely beyond the scope of this book.

However, two years later, we find representatives of the same colonies, and many of them the very same men declaring Independence. Again, bear in mind that, as pointed out earlier, many of these were the same men. Independence was actually voted on in Congress on July 2, 1776, but the document was signed on July 4. Despite the human tendency to stick to a previously decided policy, they were now declaring such reconciliation no longer possible. There is no question that this was a major shift, and even stated as such in the Declaration, saying "Prudence, indeed, will dictate that Governments long established should not be changed for light and transient causes; and accordingly all experience hath shewn, that mankind are more disposed to suffer, while evils are sufferable, than to right themselves by abolishing the forms to which they are accustomed." They certainly did not declare this independence lightly. Biographies of the participants describe the vigorous debates between those that still wished to make all attempts possible to reconcile, and those that had already given up such a hope.

Comparing the Articles of Association to the Declaration of Independence, one would think that they were written by completely different people. We already know that this is largely inaccurate. Gone was the conciliatory tone from the prior document. Where the former document made no mention of the King's role in the grievances, the Declaration of Independence was entirely personal, and doesn't mention Parliament at all. Starting with the personal accusation that "The history of the present King of Great Britain is a history of repeated injuries and usurpations", it details a list of grievances, no less than eighteen of which begin with the word "*He*." The conclusion of this list is no less personal, and is clearly judgmental, "A Prince whose character is thus marked by every act which may define a Tyrant, is unfit to be the ruler of a free people." Certainly none of the signers could expect mercy from the King should the revolution fail.

As we know, the colonies were already the targets of destructive military action by the British. It is likely that each of the representatives realized that it could still get worse, and that is certainly why many were reluctant to take this course in the first place. This document seems to go far beyond what was necessary to actually be a formal declaration of a political separation, as the minimum would have been to merely declare it so without reason. In fact, Independence was voted on and adopted on July 2, 1776, and it was only as an afterthought that they decided to put something in writing at all. As far as the contents of the document, certainly the King would either know the reasons already, or would not accept them merely because they were placed in writing. It is a valid question to ask why they would make such accusations in this document at all, since they could bring no improvement to the relationship with Britain, and would probably incite an even more forceful response. In fact, they realized that they could only be viewed as traitors to the Crown, and this list of personal accusations followed by an insult would only be likely to increase the British desire to see them all hang. It certainly suggests the question of why they would go to all this trouble.

Rather than being a simple record of their declaration, it was a carefully drafted open letter to the world, particularly to France and Spain, who still maintained their own colonial interests in the Americas. One of the reasons that some were reluctant to declare this independence was because of uncertainty about the reaction of the other great powers. Having basically no land forces, and a navy only in name, they needed to know that if they must have war with Britain, at least it would be only Britain. This explains the opening paragraph, particularly "..a decent respect to the opinions of mankind requires that they should declare the causes which impel them to the separation." They were keenly aware that their legitimacy lay in making their moral case logically to the world, because a government based on the idea that "Governments are instituted among Men, deriving their just powers from the consent of the governed" was radically different from the European paradigm. In addition, they were not fully confident in their ability to defend their legitimacy on the battlefield.

In addition to making their case against Britain by listing their specific grievances, these other nations could also be convinced that this bid for independence would not be applicable to their own colonies. The Declaration is not an invalidation of the entire concept of colonies in general, it is a statement that the King's mishandling of their specific relationship justified a severance. By laying out their specific case against the King, they could reassure France and Spain that they could support this severance without negating their own claims of authority in the New World. A further examination of those specific grievances will be more useful when discussing the later documents.

The full meaning of the independence claimed could not be clearer. In the opening paragraph, "to assume among the powers of the earth, the separate and equal station to which the Laws of Nature and of Nature's God entitle them" is an assertion that this independence makes the newly separated the political equals of any of the European powers. That this is claimed individually if in unity by each of the former colonies as new States is evident in the final paragraph, "That these United Colonies are, and of Right ought to be Free and Independent States." This reference to themselves in the plural is repeated several times in the lines that follow; "that they are Absolved from all Allegiance to the British Crown, and that all political connection between them and the State of Great Britain, is and ought to be totally dissolved; and that as Free and Independent States, they have full Power to levy War, conclude Peace, contract Alliances, establish Commerce, and to do all other Acts and Things which Independent States may of right do." It does not refer to the "United States" in the singular, not even once. The independence claimed was claimed by each colony separately, not collectively.

This is an important point to consider. As of this independence, there was no collective government of the united states, nor is there any reference to one. Each state was separate and independent, and the Continental Congress was without power to function as supreme in any way. That authority, whatever it might have been, was to be subsequently created under the Articles of Confederation, and later the Constitution. All that Congress could do was to deliberate, and to publish any collective result of that action, as assented to by representatives of the newly sovereign states. They had no authority to tax, spend, regulate or forbid anything. The Federal government did not exist.

# CHAPTER FOUR

## The Articles Of Confederation

Following the Declaration of Independence, the Continental Congress continued to meet and the two primary topics of discussion were certainly 1) how to resist the continued attempts by the British to suppress the rebellion, and 2) how the continent would move forward, assuming success of the first.

Neither was a certainty by any means. The status of the delegates and the authority of the Congress needs to be clearly understood at this point. The delegates had been chosen by their States, but this did not give the collective body any specific power over the States as a whole. Not only were the delegates of the various States aware that they could lose the war, they realized that the withdrawal of one or more from their rebellion by making separate reconciliations with Britain would have disastrous results on those remaining. As desirable as holding together was to them all, it was not taken for granted by any.

The difficulty of pursuing these simultaneous objectives resulted in it requiring over a year to finalize the Articles of Confederation, in 1777, which were fully ratified in 1781. It needs to be borne in mind while considering the contents and effects of this document that the war would continue until the Treaty of Paris in 1783.

The Articles of Confederation was the first document to create the federal government, and it is worth reiterating that it was created by representatives of sovereign entities who were under no obligation to agree to anything. The opening paragraph does contain the phrase "perpetual union", but the document is a clear definition of what that union includes and what it does not.

The first article simply names the union as the United States of America, and that is of course the most logical thing for the document to do first.

In the second, there is a clear statement that the document does not relinquish the sovereignty of the States, and that any power not delegated to the new federal body was retained by the several States. Although they were agreeing to a permanent union, it was a union within certain specific parameters and purposes.

The first purpose so listed was, as would be expected under the circumstances of being at war to defend the very sovereignty they claimed in both the Declaration of Independence and in Article Two, a pledge of mutual support for the purpose of military defense.

Next was a pledge to respect each others' citizens and rules of law, including treating citizens of other states equally to their own, and assisting the enforcement of decisions of each others' civil and criminal courts. Like several provisions of the Articles of Confederation, the "full faith and credit" clause appearing here was imported into the Constitution later.

Representatives to the Congress were to be chosen by the States, subject to recall by the States, and to be maintained (paid) by the States. At this point, there was no mention of this body representing the People of their State, this Congress was a collection of representatives of the States as States. Congress was not so much the government itself, but representatives of the individual States TO that government. As such, they were prohibited from simultaneously holding any salaried federal position while acting as representatives of their State. The only other limitation on who could be a representative was that no one could serve for more than three out of six years.

Article 8 seeks to limit the independence of each State in regards to military buildup, foreign relations, and trade protectionism. It clearly reserves the making of foreign friendships to the federal body, particularly the eventual treaty to end the ongoing war, and attempts to strike a balance between discouraging a State from building an aggressive capacity on their own and allowing them to maintain that which would be necessary for their own defense. At the same time, it placed a requirement, if difficult to quantify, that each state maintain the ability to contribute military power to a common defense.

Other than charging for postage to defray the cost of operating a mail service, Congress was limited in raising of revenue to a property tax on the value of land, collection of which remained the responsibility of the State where such property was located.

One interesting provision was the complete absence of a formal recognized judiciary for disputes between states, that judicial function being served on an ad hoc basis by members of Congress selected by a rather convoluted multi-step process.

Future admission of other States was foreseen, and would have to be approved by the member states, except for Canada which was "pre-approved."

A provision that did cause some problems was the acceptance of the "war debt" of the several States. While the war expenditures in pursuit of independence would clearly be valid, this particular provision only addressed those that had incurred debts. Some had paid cash out of their own treasuries, and probably were less than enthusiastic about effectively paying for the war twice.

Where the Articles of Confederation doomed itself to ultimate failure, even thought it was replaced by the Constitution before the problem arose, was in the final provision. It required any change to be passed by Congress, and then ratified by every member State. Because additional states joining later was already foreseen, this was going to cause conflicts in the execution of several other provisions that required the agreement of nine of the States, because it would not take many additional members for that number to no longer represent a majority.

All in all, the Articles of Confederation created a very clear limited common government. It's only powers were in areas of contact between the States as States, to avoid conflict among themselves, as a body to resolve any such conflicts as were otherwise unavoidable, and in relations to foreign powers, either as a source of unified authority for conducting war, or as a unified voice of diplomacy to avoid it, and particularly to ultimately conclude the ongoing war.

There was no mention of individual rights and freedoms, as there was no nexus between individuals and the federal government. The individual needed only to concern himself with his relationship to the government of the State where he lived. Any impact of the federal government on a private citizen would be required to go through their State government, and even the limitations on accepting any titles and gifts from foreign governments was applicable only to those who were members of Congress.

The Articles of Confederation was a compact between the States, and there was no involvement of or authority over individual citizens.

# CHAPTER FIVE

## The Constitution, An Overview

In this chapter, we'll examine the Preamble, and a few other selected parts of the Constitution. What I intend to prove in this part is that YOU can read and understand the document. Again, I'm not going to add any words to the document, or invent new definitions for the words, or even talk about what might "emanate from a penumbra" within the Constitution. All I will do is point to a few specific sections, and the logical conclusions will be obvious. Everything we need to know is in the Constitution itself, but it sometimes helps to read certain parts out of order.

First, let's look at the Preamble in some detail.

We the People of the United States, in Order to form a more perfect Union, establish Justice, insure domestic Tranquility, provide for the common defence, promote the general Welfare, and secure the Blessings of Liberty to ourselves and our Posterity, do ordain and establish this Constitution for the United States of America.

Notice that the Preamble is a single sentence. Understanding it is as simple as any other sentence, you simply need to break it down into its component parts. With apologies to every English teacher I ever had, the three parts are Who, What, and Why. We are going to examine it and look for Who is doing something, What are they doing, and Why are they doing it.

"We the People of the United States" is the Who, it identifies the producers of this document, it is their statement of authority. The document is not being forced upon the People, it was created by representatives of the People to create the Constitution in their name. The document itself is of you. It was written on your behalf, on your authority. We're going to discuss this phrase again in the next chapter.

The What is the last phrase `do ordain and establish this Constitution for the United States of America.` What the Constitution does is create the government. While the government did actually already exist (such as it was) under the Articles of Confederation, the document following this Preamble will define it. We shall see later what degree of specificity there is in the definition, or if it is vague, flexible, and subject to interpretation. In the name of the People, the government is created. The government does not create itself, nor is it created by any foreign source, and all argument over whether the Framers of the Constitution were Christians or Atheists are moot, as it is not done by claim of or in denial of any Divine Right.

Everything in between is the Why. We'll examine the list more closely later, but one of the items is to `secure the Blessings of Liberty.`

So the basic meaning of the Preamble is that the People establish the government of the United States, according to that which follows, for the purpose of protecting their own Freedom. We will explore several logical implications of the Preamble later, but the main one to grasp right now is this: In the body of the document following is a description of the federal government, including authority, power, obligations, and limitations.

Now let's explore the authority of the People to actually do this, including how a group of 54 men could actually draft such a document in their name. The answer to this is found in Article Seven. `The Ratification of the Conventions of nine States, shall be sufficient for the Establishment of this Constitution between the States so ratifying the Same.` What that means is that had only eight states ratified it in a convention of delegates chosen by their own People, it would have had no effect at all. The Framers wrote it in the name of the People, but even after they were finished, the document itself required the approval of the states to be effective. As History did unfold, it was not unanimously accepted; many of the votes to ratify it were very close, and some took longer than others. In the end, though, this Constitution was accepted by the People, and is therefore OF the People.

A further point to recall is that it was the Framers' idea that this government, whatever it would be, would be one of the Peoples' choosing. Remember the Declaration of Independence, which states "Governments are instituted among Men, deriving their just powers from the consent of the governed" and "... it is the Right of the People to ... institute new Government, laying its foundation on such principles and organizing its powers in such form, as to them shall seem most likely to effect their Safety and Happiness." Whatever government they created, they knew they needed the consent of the People.

Now, let's turn our attention to the question of what the nature of the government they were creating was to be. Going back to the Why of the Preamble, we see "in Order to form a more perfect Union, establish Justice, insure domestic Tranquility, provide for the common defence, promote the general Welfare, and secure the Blessings of Liberty to ourselves and our Posterity." There are six items here, and while this is one part of the Constitution that may seem somewhat vague, one needs to bear in mind that this is nothing more than a statement of purpose. It is not a grant of authority. The authority comes later, and what the various grants of authority contain will resolve any remaining doubts as to the statement of purpose.

"[A] more perfect Union" refers back to the Articles of Confederation. There were some serious problems with the central government under the Articles of Confederation, and the delegates were actually charged with fixing that document, not creating something totally new. Be that as it may, they did create a new document, and the People accepted it, so if they were technically guilty of exceeding their authority, they have been absolved by the ratification of the Constitution. Their stated intention to "establish Justice, insure domestic Tranquility" referred largely to the lack of a uniform system of courts, and in the tendency of the state legislatures to often fail to protect private property. "[P]romote the general Welfare" may appear somewhat vague, but the concept is directly connected to "and secure the Blessings of Liberty." Referring back to the Declaration of Independence again, we can get an idea of what they thought these blessings were: "Life, Liberty, and the pursuit of Happiness."

So, the Preamble says that this is a document of the People, and that's reinforced by the requirement that the People accept it for it to become operative. It also asserts that the purpose is to preserve the Liberty of the People. It only stands to reason that the People would be more likely to accept it (in other words, vote to ratify it and make it effective) if they understood it, especially in that era. If the voting public were at all doubtful, they would be more prone to reject it, given that a major war had just been fought to rid themselves of a government whose workings they could not control. They certainly would not agree to one they couldn't even understand.

As it was, ratification was a difficult task. Improving the likelihood of success was the entire point of the *Federalist Papers*, which were a series of newspaper articles, intended for the general (voting) public to read and consider. I will not be going into their content at this time, mostly because a) they are not the Constitution itself, and b) their intended audience was for people who had already read the document in the first place, and c) they were written afterward, so the proper time to discuss their content would be after we have read the document itself.

Now, having leaped from the Preamble to the last Article, let us make another leap, this time to the Tenth Amendment.

*"Amendment 10*

*The powers not delegated to the United States by the Constitution, nor prohibited by it to the States, are reserved to the States respectively, or to the people."*

This is an important provision, but in most ordinary contracts, one that would not be necessary. If you were to contract to buy a boat, you would not be able to assume that the contract includes the trailer it sits on unless the contract specifically says it is included. However, since the People had a reasonable mistrust of government in general, this provision was generally demanded, along with the rest of the Bill of Rights, beginning before the ratification of the seven Articles was even complete, in order to make it clear that government had no power not specifically granted to it.

What makes this provision so important, despite it being arguably unnecessary, is that it makes it crystal clear that the Constitution has a firm, fixed, and absolute meaning. If you will recall back in Chapter One, I promised to prove that it did. That's your proof.

Now, I want to discuss two other concepts before we move on to the actual contents of the Constitution. One is another fallacy that may have prevented you from reading it, the other is the last of the statements I asked you to take on faith in the beginning.

We've all heard it said that the Constitution is a "living, breathing" document. Most of the time people say that, they are justifying the concept that it is flexible, and can expand with the needs of modern society, which is true. What is not true is the means by which these same people generally allege that it lives and breathes.

Article Five describes the correct procedure to alter the Constitution. This very clearly shows an intent that the meaning and effect of the Constitution be firm and fixed, and if it proved unworkable, Article Five creates a mechanism to change it. If it needs to change, it can change without impairing the parts that still work, but it must be by the agreement of three quarters of the states. Particularly in the light of Amendment Ten, it is easy to see that if the Constitution is to change, the People must be consulted on the matter, and overwhelmingly agree to it. It simply is not left up to any branch of the federal government itself to stretch the Constitution in any way. The meaning of the Constitution is unchanging, unless changed by a validly adopted Amendment under Article Five. No one else has the authority to change it.

Not counting the First Ten Amendments, it has been successfully used to add seventeen such Amendments, including one that reversed an earlier one (Prohibition). This suggests that if the Constitution is in any sense "Living", that the mechanism found here is what gives it the ability to grow with changing times and technologies. Were the Constitution vague and flexible enough to allow the government itself to redefine the extent of powers granted as it saw fit, there would be no need for this Article Five.

We have seen through our overview of History and the words in the Preamble that the purpose of the Constitution was to protect the Liberty of the People. We have seen that one of the greatest threats to that Liberty was seen as government itself, and that the Framers were careful to be clear that the government was not empowered to change the terms of the Constitution.

However, there is one point still missing, one important

factor to the Constitution that needs to be very clearly understood. Even if we all agree that the purpose of the Constitution was to define a limited federal government, and deny it the power to expand its own power and thereby be capable of becoming tyrannical, we have to recognize that there is no set of words that could accomplish this without regular oversight by the beneficiaries of the intended protection. In other words... if the People no longer know what the Constitution says, it cannot protect them from anything.

For the Constitution to serve its purpose of protecting citizens against tyranny, the people have to read it. The People also have to demand that the government abide by it, but that is only possible if sufficient numbers of the People actually have read it.

For a government whose legitimate authority derives from the governed to function and remain within the legitimate boundaries so established, those boundaries must be familiar to the majority of the citizens. If the Founding Fathers knew this, then they surely strove to write in a manner that required no special education to understand, and intended to be extremely precise.

# CHAPTER SIX

## The Preamble, In Greater Detail

The Preamble to the Constitution begins with the words "We, the People." Never before was a government so created. Even the Magna Carta was a document limiting the King's authority over the powers of the Nobles, and as such had nothing to do with the People. The first three of the Great Documents were done in the name of the Colonies/States. This was the first time in History that the common man has had a government instituted in their own name.

The Articles of Association was presented as a document produced by delegates, acting in their capacity as delegates of the Colonies. The Declaration of Independence was "of the thirteen united States of America", not the People of those States. The Articles of Confederation begins "To all to whom these Presents shall come, we the undersigned Delegates of the States affixed to our Names send greeting." The Constitution is unique because it is a document that establishes a government on the basis of the authority of the People of the country. As we saw in the Declaration of Independence, governments are "instituted among Men, deriving their just powers from the consent of the governed", so it naturally follows that the government should have been created on the authority of the People, rather than by the government itself. Even so, it makes the Constitution a unique document, even among American documents.

That's an enormous difference. Instead of being a document presented TO the People, this document purports to be an act OF the People. This signals an awareness, which may have been less prevalent in the creation of the documents which went before, of the interests of the average person in this government being created. Given the experience of the People with governments up to that time, which we know from the outline of History in general, and the documents presented previously in particular, we would expect that the document produced by the People which creates yet another government would have several characteristics, which we could easily imagine with just a moment's reflection, given the Historic nature of the time in which it was written.

Naturally, the People would want the government's ability to interfere with their lives to be minimized. If we were to compare the Declaration of Independence with the Constitution (which we will), we would expect to find the government clearly forbidden to do most, if not all of those things that they had listed as grievances leading to the separation in the first place.

If the purpose of the document is to bind the federal government from undue interference with the lives of the People, it is only logical to expect that the document would be written in simple enough language that it would be understandable by anyone reasonably literate. That's the whole point of this book.

The structure of the government so created will have many safeguards to avoid concentrations of power, not the least of which is some direct control by the People over the government itself. This would be a change from the Congress up to that time being representatives of the Colonies or States, and simply making rules for the People to adhere to. If it is the People creating the government, we would expect to see limitations on what the government created can do, and maybe even limitations on what the States are allowed to do, but we would not expect there to be many requirements and obligations placed on the People themselves, if any at all.

It would most certainly be clear. If the object is that this document is to protect individual liberty from an excessive government, then any such document written by the People would be clear where the limitations on government action are placed. It has been stated by various persons at various times that the Constitution is a "living document", by which those persons mean that it can be stretched to allow the government to do things that it doesn't appear to allow. Since we now have the concept of what the document is, and have some appreciation from prior chapters of the length of time it took to produce the document, we know instinctively that this cannot be true. There was no built-in vagueness to the document, that's why they built-in a specific procedure (Article 5) for Amending it should that be seen as necessary. Had the intent been to create a government which is self-defining, there would have been no need to write anything at all. If the powers of the federal government needed to be flexible, then certainly the Articles of Confederation could have been stretched and adjusted and deemed to permit the existing Congress to do what they felt was needed, had the single body of government that was the Congress under the Articles of Confederation found it appropriate. However, it's simply impossible to reconcile the thought of a "self-defining government" with the knowledge that these same authors had just fought a war to relieve themselves of another government that had done precisely that.

Another thing that would occur to us to expect would be that the basic nature of the government the document creates should be evident in the document itself, and would be categorized one of two ways: Either the People would be looking to government to solve a wide variety of problems of the People, in which case the government would be clearly charged with solving them as a responsibility, or they would be cautious about creating a government with the power to annoy them to the extent that Britain had. If the People are writing the document, then it would either create barriers to protect them from that government, or it would create a powerful government intended to serve them as a whole. You may judge for yourself which of those two possibilities is apparent in the document itself.

The Preamble continues, crediting several purposes for the document itself. These purposes are largely already familiar to us from reading the previous documents. If we had thought that the United States was being created for the first time by the Constitution, the phrase "more perfect union" might make us wonder, "more perfect than what?" but we know the answer, "more perfect than that which the Articles of Confederation provided."

"Justice" harkens back to several of the complaints of the Declaration of Independence, including trials taking place at distances inconvenient for Defendants or victims of crimes, and tyrannical disrespect for private properties. It goes hand in hand with the document coming from "The People", and giving them a more direct voice in the government is one of the ways to make it a more Just system. It also has application, even if it doesn't refer to, the provision of the Articles that gave each state an equal voice in the federal government. There were those that felt number of inhabitants should impact representation, so the "one state, one vote" was felt to be an injustice to the more populous areas. Also, Justice is involved in the part of the Constitution that deals with the concepts of extradition between States.

Apparently, the imperfections of the government under the Articles created some differences among the States, so a new Constitution was drafted to promote "domestic tranquility", while the whole purpose of the Union in the first place was mutual Defense. As "promoting the general welfare" was probably intended, that certainly had more to do with inter-State trade and development of the economy of the whole than with redistribution of income.

# CHAPTER SEVEN

## The Articles

Having the proper background in History, and in the purpose and limitations provided previously, you are almost ready to read the Constitution on your own. A few more notes to facilitate the reading still remain.

Remember that despite all the History and other documents that we've looked at, the Constitution is all there is to say about the structure and power of the Federal government. The other documents are interesting, informative, and will facilitate your understanding, but the Constitution stands alone, unmodified by them.

While the Preamble is important, you have to realize that the operative provisions are found in the Articles of the Constitution, as Amended by the Amendments. The Amendments are also important, as we have already seen just by taking a look at the Tenth Amendment out of sequence. For the moment, you are safe in ignoring them entirely, and getting an understanding of the original Constitution as written. You have to start someplace, and I believe that to start with the Amendments increases the likelihood that what you see will confuse you. I think it is better to start with the original document, and later analyze each Amendment for what it changes.

The body of the Constitution is presented in seven Articles. This is where we will find the effects of the Document, whatever they might be. We have already discussed the Seventh and Fifth earlier. The first three are our subject at hand.

The federal government as created by the Articles of Confederation had a single body, whose members were entirely under the control of the States. The fact that the entire Constitution is claimed to be a product of the People should keep us from being surprised that the new federal government would contain members who were selected by, and representing the interests of the People that chose them.

The government created was (and largely still is) comprised of three separate and distinct branches. The first to be considered was the Legislature, under Article I. This is what one might expect to come first, being that they were basically defining what their successors in function would be, but more importantly, because the Judiciary and Executive branches would be defined at least in part in terms of their roles regarding actions after the Legislature had made decisions, or in some cases receive their authority from the Legislature. Defining the Legislature first was probably the best way to make the other components easily comprehensible.

The creation of Congress in two bodies was a reflection on the fact that they recognized that the People as individuals had a stake in the federal government, but also recognized that the States were still sovereign entities, at least up until the ratification of the Constitution, and each must have their own separate voice in the Legislature.

The minimum requirements for each house were few. Both were given a minimum age, the Senate's being higher, but how individuals were chosen was not left up to the States. One was chosen by a direct vote of the People, and not the States, while the Senate was to be chosen by the Legislature of the States, and not the People nor by the exclusive act of a Governor or other executive. The number of Representatives from each State was based on population numbers, but each State received an equal number of Senators.

The actual grant of power, other than to try Impeachments, appears in Article I, Section 8. Bear in mind what we already saw in the Tenth Amendment, which tells us that they are only granted the authority given, and no more. For example, they receive the authority to promote Art and Science, but their authority is specifically limited to granting Copyrights and Patents. In light of the Tenth Amendment, that doesn't appear to extend to providing any kind of subsidy for either. As you read through Article I, it should be apparent that there are no occasions where the government is empowered to act where federal involvement would be a surprise to the average citizen, even if had they not read the Constitution.

I expect many people to become confused even just reading Article I, as it would appear that many things the federal government is doing are not enumerated. Many of these are activities that have been unquestioned for decades, even generations. The human tendency is to want to reconcile such a contradiction, and the simplest way is to conclude that the individual simply cannot understand the document, and that the government must be correct. Remember that the logical deductions that come from the phrase "We, the People" demand that the government be comprehensible to you. Many of the discrepancies are explainable, and many are explained in various opinions of the Courts. These, too, must be comprehensible to the citizen to be valid. Were it otherwise, we would still have a self-defining government, rendering the entire Constitution a pointless exercise in futility.

I warned you that you were going to have to be willing to consider a whole new paradigm, and to declare that "the Emperor is naked." If you are seeing things the federal government is doing that are not permitted under the Constitution, you may or may not be correct, but you are certainly entitled to an adequate explanation.

Article Two creates the Presidency. Much of the Article describes how the President is chosen. The most notable aspect of this part is that it gives the power to select the people who will choose the President to the States as States, and doesn't give the People any direct control, and only the remotest of indirect control over the process. It doesn't forbid the States from giving it to the People, but it clearly does not anticipate that, as the office wasn't foreseen to have any direct impact on the People.

One of the matters that is frequently discussed but absent from the Constitution is "Presidential Succession." If it should happen that both the President and Vice-President were unable to serve as President, the Constitution does not directly answer the question of who would act in their place. Article Two, Section 1, Clause 6 empowers Congress to make that determination, which they did in the Presidential Succession Act of 1947.

The President is empowered to make appointments, and to suggest things to Congress, and is the Commander in Chief. As described in the Constitution, there isn't a lot of autonomy to the office, most of what he does is follow the instructions of Congress, and at least get their input on what he does on his own.

The Constitution only creates a single Court, and it specifies what kind of cases they may hear, and the few that can only be brought directly to them. All other courts are created by Congress under the authority granted to them to create such courts.

One thing to notice here is that Supreme Court Justices are appointed for Life, but that is followed by "during good behavior." This suggests that it is at least theoretically possible to Impeach a sitting Supreme Court Justice. Although this has never been seriously attempted, it appears to have been contemplated by the authors.

The Jurisdiction of the Supreme Court is limited. Basically, they can only hear cases that are not strictly internal to States, and in many of those cases they can hear, can only hear them on Appeal from a lower court. This limitation on jurisdiction to exclude internal state matters, such as criminal laws, goes hand in hand with the concept of the States as sovereigns. The USSC has no authority to control intrastate matters, because the Constitution lacks the power to give it any. It is only where states or the citizens thereof come in contact with other states, or foreign governments, that there is any authority.

It certainly appears from reading the first three Articles that they are very specific about what each branch was intended to do. The fact that they organized the Constitution into a single Article for each of them suggests they were attempting to be organized and make the document easier to understand. If there were something to include about the President, it went into Article Two, and if it were about the Congress, it went into Article One. Were this not the case, it would be hard to explain why there were separate and distinct Articles for each branch.

Article Four deals with relationships between the States, and Article Six has very little importance in modern times, as it was a housekeeping provision to settle debts of the federal government, incurred prior to the adoption of the Constitution. Article Seven is the validation procedure, which once completed, has little forward application.

Now, it is time for you to turn to Appendix Four and read the Constitution from start to finish.

# CHAPTER EIGHT

## The Bill Of Rights

The Bill of Rights, as you probably know, is the collective name for the first ten Amendments to the Constitution. It is important to understand the time line for them, just as it was to understand the Constitution.

The Constitution was drafted in 1787. It was ratified by the nine states required for it to take effect in 1788, with the last to do so being Rhode Island, in 1790. During the extensive debates, speeches, and newspaper articles and editorials on the subject, one of the issues was distrust due to the lack of inclusion of any mention of individual rights. The Bill of Rights was drafted in 1789, and ultimately ratified in 1791. These appear in Appendix 5. It is useful to bear in mind that the Bill of Rights, like the Constitution itself, only applies to the federal government (we'll get to the 14th Amendment later), unless clearly stated otherwise.

It is worth noting, at least in passing, that two other proposed amendments were not ratified with the Bill of Rights, one concerning the ratio of constituents per each Representative, and the other affecting compensation of Congressmen. The latter was ultimately ratified, in 1992, and is the 27th Amendment.

Most of the first eight are easily recognizable as among the grievances and problems that the entire revolution sought to relieve. The important thing to bear in mind is that the Ninth Amendment clearly states that it is not an exhaustive list. We already discussed the significance of the Tenth.

The First Amendment's first clause is the one most often discussed, "Congress shall make no law respecting an establishment of religion, or prohibiting the free exercise thereof."

Whatever it says, it is directed at Congress, that's pretty clear. What is missing, however, is the phrase "separation of church and state." While a lot of time has been spent discussing the meaning of "separation of church and state", apparently no one has noticed its absence.

While most of the founding fathers were Christians, and many were actually members of the clergy, there was no single division of Christianity that predominated. Many of them had originally left England, or their recent ancestors had done so, to find a place to be free to worship as they chose. Had they been of a mind to establish a national religion along with the federal government, it is unlikely that the Constitution would have ever gained approval even of the body of authors, let alone the People. The idea in the First Amendment was to prevent the government from giving a monopoly to one religion, or outlawing another. It by no means went any farther than that. "In God We Trust" on our currency doesn't respect any specific religion, nor does it forbid another. The presence of the Ten Commandments doesn't respect any specific religion, nor forbid another.

Up until the end of the war by the Treaty of Paris in 1783, many colonists, in particular those who had signed the Declaration of Independence, were concerned with being labeled as traitors to England for having, speaking, or printing opposing views. One method to stifle both the rebellion and the colonists' government was for the Crown to outlaw assemblies of the people, and to control what could be printed and distributed. The final part harkens back to the reference in the Declaration of Independence where their petition to relieve their disagreements were totally ignored.

Taken as a whole, the First Amendment recognizes the right to think differently, and express opposing views and ideas.

The Second Amendment is one of the most simple provisions of the entire document. "A well regulated

Militia, being necessary to the security of a free State, the right of the people to keep and bear Arms shall not be infringed."
The way to make it clear is to parse the sentence grammatically. If you do that, it becomes clear that it really doesn't matter what a "militia" is or was, and it doesn't really matter if one is necessary for anything. What matters is the operative provision, which is the expression of the Right itself. It fails to specify who is prohibited from infringing that Right, unlike the First Amendment which is directed at Congress, which appears to mean that the Right is guaranteed against anybody.

Again we turn to History to understand why they thought that was important. The Declaration of Independence spoke of a right to abolish a government that no longer served its proper function, but this would be impossible to do if that government had the monopoly on weaponry. The first act of the English when they decided to take military action had been to attempt to seize the armories at Lexington and Concord. The Second Amendment has no less of a meaning than to forbid the government from stripping the people of the right to own the means of opposing by force a government that has gone beyond "the consent of the governed."

Another point to bear in mind is that even if the Second Amendment only applies to the right of a "Militia" to be armed, the Ninth might well apply to the same right for individuals as an "unenumerated right."

The Third Amendment has sometimes been said to be the only one that the federal government has never violated. To understand why it is here is easy for someone who read through the list of complaints in the Declaration of Independence, or considered the Intolerable Acts previously mentioned. Remember that one of the Intolerable Acts was that the English claimed the right to house the troops sent to the Colonies in buildings owned by private citizens. No report of occupants actually being ejected are known, but the fact that the right was claimed was so abhorrent that many People wanted to make that clear to the new government.

The fourth, fifth, and Sixth amendments all concern citizens charged with or suspected of criminal offenses, and seek to prevent the use of government power to harass the citizens. The Fourth is probably the most often referred to. The first clause is what is protected, "The right of the people to be secure in their persons, houses, papers, and effects" appears to only contain physical objects (including the physical person), and what is prohibited includes "unreasonable searches and seizures." Of course, this is not an absolute bar to such searches and seizures, but "no Warrants shall issue, but upon probable cause, supported by Oath or affirmation" and even when they do that, they have to "particularly describe the place to be searched, and the persons or things to be seized."

It isn't difficult to see whether or not a Warrant may be issued in a particular circumstance. However, the warrant provision only applies if the government wants to do something that would otherwise be prohibited. Not everything is prohibited. If whatever is being done is not considered "unreasonable", there is no need for a warrant. An "unreasonable" search may include other circumstances not listed in the Fourth Amendment (again, see the Ninth), but minimally includes "persons, houses, papers, and effects." According to many supreme court decisions and "conventional wisdom," it also includes telephone conversations. It is obvious that the authors of the Constitution wanted to make it clear that the government could not physically interfere with an individual's home, or workplace, or their person at will, but we have to consider whether or not electronic surveillance (I doubt any of them ever considered the possibility of telephones, electronic mail, or electronic eavesdropping) would be affected, as it does not interfere with the individual. The concept of "eavesdropping" was know, and is not specifically mentioned. It is arguable that wiretapping is no different than eavesdropping. I shall leave that up to you to consider for yourself, at least until much later in this book.

The Fifth mostly contains limits on government prosecution of criminal offenses. It limits the ability of government officials to use government power to harass others with unsubstantiated charges, or to repeatedly try someone for the same crime, or to exact punishments arbitrarily. Worth noticing is that it twice refers to the possibility of the death penalty, and does not ban it outright. It also doesn't forbid government seizures, provided that the owner is compensated.

The Sixth also addresses minimum standards for treatment of criminal defendants. They did not specifically define what a "speedy trial" is, but do guarantee it. The requirement that the trial be held near where the offense occurred again hearkens back to the Intolerable Acts. This amendment is a guarantee of what has come to be known as "Due Process", which is basically a matter of attempting to neutralize the government's "home court" advantage in a criminal proceeding.

The Seventh's guarantee of a jury trial seeks to limit the power of a professional judiciary by giving the fact-finding power to a panel of citizens in all but the most petty of civil matters, and inhibiting re-examination of those facts later.

The Eighth Amendment is fairly straightforward, but it is worth noting that the prohibition against "excessive bail" does not require that all defendants be given the opportunity to post bail. Also noteworthy is that the ban on "cruel and unusual punishment" probably does not refer to capital punishment, given that capital punishment is mentioned twice in the Fifth Amendment. Obviously it limits the manner in which it could be carried out, but there is no way to declare that it prohibits the practice entirely without negating two parts of another Amendment.

# CHAPTER NINE

## Impact Of Some Of The Amendments

The Eleventh and Twelfth are interesting Amendments, in that they both reiterate state sovereignty in different ways.

The Eleventh makes it clear that the federal judiciary has no jurisdiction in a suit against a State by an individual. While it only applies to cases "at law or in equity", that means it does not bar a suit being initiated in a federal court, if brought on Constitutional grounds such as Roe v. Wade.

The Twelfth altered the procedures for Presidential Elections, leaving intact the Constitution's allowing the states complete autonomy in the method of selecting the delegates to the Electoral College. The clear implication of the overall method of choosing the President is to remove the decision by at least one layer from a direct vote of the People. States are by no means required to consult the People at all in this decision, and even in the case of there being no majority in the Electoral College, the decision goes into the House of Representatives. There is no provision for a run-off election, and no provision for a case where a state might fail to have any qualified Electors at all.

The reasoning behind the Electoral College is similar to the reason for having a Congress. The desire was to have decisions made by a smaller number than the whole, to represent the best interests of the People, even when it conflicted with their actual desires which might be based on less-well-informed passions of the moment. The numbers of Electors for each state is also similar to the reasons for having two houses of Congress, effected by basing the Electors on the authorized number of Representatives and Senators. This was to base it in part on population, and part on each having an equal voice. As it works out, it does give individual voters of some states more weight than others, but the fact is that the federal government was not intended to "serve" the demands of the People so much as it was to leave the People alone.

One thing to notice about the potential results of the procedure is that it is theoretically possible for a person to be chosen President with a single Electoral vote. If two candidates fail to capture a majority, and a third captures a single Electoral vote, the matter is decided in the House of Representatives, and they could legitimately choose the third-place finisher. As unlikely as that may be, that is the system.

The Thirteenth Amendment completely abolished Slavery. It very broadly prohibits any kind of "involuntary servitude" except as punishment for a crime. The question of whether military conscription violates this has been raised several times, once in the Supreme Court, and the decision that it does not is less than convincing. The text is quite clear, and doesn't leave any room for an exception for a war in Europe, and yet that exception was found.

The Fourteenth did several things, and has had effects far beyond what might have been intended. One of these was to make United States citizens of the former Confederate States by declaring anyone born in the US a US citizen, but its effect now is that persons here illegally who give birth are the parents of a US citizen. This Amendment is what has been used to interpret selected portions of the Bill of Rights as being limitations of State actions, not just federal. Sections 3 and 4 very clearly are intended to disallow any politician in office at the time of the Civil War from ever holding office again (unless specifically allowed to by Congress), and deny the validity of any debt owed by the Confederacy, or loss suffered because of the emancipation of slaves. It would appear that this was the last time the United States seemed to know exactly what to do after winning a war.

The Fifteenth prohibits limiting the right to vote based on race. The Constitution is actually silent on qualifications to vote prior to this. Up to this point, States retained the power to decide what qualified a person to vote. Some States did have laws that prevented blacks from voting, but not all did.

The Sixteenth allows Income Taxes. Unfortunately, this Amendment puts no limitation on how much can be demanded. It is unique in that it is the first mention in the Constitution of a power of the federal government over individuals, and also because that power has no limitations.

The Seventeenth has caused more trouble than many realize. Prior to it, the selection of Senators was controlled by Article I, Section 3, which requires that they be "chosen by the Legislature" of the State they are to represent. The original purpose of the Senate was to represent States as Independent Sovereign States, and with the passage of this Amendment, they would no longer do that. Erosion of State authority in favor of greater federal power would be unchallenged, as they were answerable to the People, not the States themselves. The Constitution originally broke the Congress into two houses for the purpose of giving the People representation in Congress while retaining that of the States. This Amendment has the effect of making the States subject to a government in which they have no guarantee of a voice.

The Eighteenth initiated the Prohibition, the 21st ended it. I have no explanation of why the federal government needed this Amendment in 1917 control alcohol, but doesn't need it to control "drugs."

The Nineteenth granted the vote to women, equal to men. Again, no such prohibition in the Constitution ever existed, this prohibited States from denying women the right to vote. It is interesting to note that women in New Jersey were allowed to vote (and apparently did) due to their State Constitution granting the vote to "all inhabitants", until that was amended in 1807.

The Twentieth affected timing of changing over the Presidency, and required Congress to meet at least once per year. This is probably the only provision in the entire Constitution that would present less of a danger if it were violated than observed.

The 22d Amendment limits any individual from being elected to President more than twice. It is interesting that the People are having this choice taken from them, and yet they were given the control over the Senate. Also, the number of terms one may serve in the office of President is limited, but no other office is so limited. Remember that the Articles of Confederation prohibited anyone from serving more than three of any six years in that Congress. This would probably be unnecessary if the Constitutional limitations on Presidential Powers were actually enforced.

The 23d Amendment gave the District of Columbia some of the political advantages of being a state without becoming a state. Prior to this, only states had any influence over who would be President, or have representation in Congress. It is another milestone in our journey from being a voluntary union of states to a federal government, subdivided into states for its convenience.

The 24th prohibited barring People from voting by requiring a tax to be paid.

The 25th provides for cases where the President is unable to act as President, and resolution of a difference of opinion on that issue between the President and anyone else.

In the 26th, the federal government once again stepped in to decide who could vote within the states, this time, extending the right to persons 18 or older.

The 27th is a subtle change, where previously no pay raises for congress could take effect for a specific person until they were re-elected, this states that pay raises have to wait until a new House of Representatives is elected. Since that happens every two years, and Senators serve for six, that probably had the Senate's overwhelming support. It is interesting to notice that this makes the United States

Congress the only people in the country who have the power to control their own salaries, including business owners, who need the consent of customers.

# CHAPTER TEN

## Comments On The Federalist Papers

There are two points I'd like you to remember when reading this chapter. One is that I personally have the utmost respect for the Federalist Papers, its authors and contents. The other is that my purpose in this chapter is to convince you that you don't need to read them to understand the Constitution, while not discouraging you from doing so. I'm not trying to keep you from reading them, I just want you to put them into their proper perspective when it comes to knowing what's in the Constitution.

The Federalist Papers are generally considered to be the province of Constitutional Experts, in that most people presume that one cannot be considered an "expert" on the Constitution without an intimacy with their contents. I do not agree with this contention in the least. In fact, as I have indicated before, I don't really recognize that there are "experts" on the Constitution, one has either read it or they haven't; all the extra material one might read to become an "expert" merely makes one expert in the subject of "other material written about the Constitution." The Federalist Papers fall into that category.

Let me be clear that I do not mean to criticize or minimize the value of them. They are an extraordinary work, with inestimable value for several purposes. They lay out the case for a central government in the first place, and discuss aspects of that which the Constitution contains, they give a very clear indication of what the framers had in mind, what they wanted to avoid, and what they thought the result of inaction would be. Very clearly their contents will afford one a much deeper understanding of the Constitution.

In addition to being "about the Constitution", they

have also been praised as a scholarly work on politics and government in general, and it cannot be disputed that the authors were experts on that subject, very likely having no equals in the twenty-first century. This, they very clearly are, giving reference and comments on the effects of political organizations that many people have never heard of, let alone studied to the extent that these three obviously had.

A modern reader needs to bear in mind that when originally written, they were a series of newspaper articles (published under pseudonyms), written to convince the voters of New York to adopt the Constitution. Given that the first 36 articles were first published in March of 1788, and that six of the States had already ratified them by that time, it's obvious that most of the voters in most states had to make their decision without them. My point here is that you can, too.

You should also bear in mind that what is now considered a "scholarly work" was originally intended for the ordinary individual of 1788.

One other point to be aware of is that, owing to their nature as persuasive writing, they tend to present only one side of an argument, and that their very existence implies that there is another side, possibly multiple sides. The Federalist Papers were written in support of the adoption of the Constitution, and we must at least consider the possibility that there might be other points in opposition, even beyond those that they might address. There most certainly were opponents of even the idea of unifying the thirteen States into a single government, some of whom favored Confederations of two to four States, or each State retaining complete and total autonomy and independence from all others. In fact, approximately the first half of the Federalist Papers is dedicated to defending the idea of a single Union, without any particular emphasis on the nature of the Union being that which the (proposed) Constitution specifically provides.

However, they are not at all required reading to be able to understand the Constitution's provisions as written, and moreover, nothing in them will change what is in the Constitution.

The Federalist Papers are a collection of 85 articles that were published in the newspapers in an effort to persuade the voters of New York to adopt the Constitution. Each was written by one of three men, James Madison, who later became President, John Jay, who became the first Chief Justice of the Supreme Court, and Alexander Hamilton, the first Secretary of the Treasury. Distinguished as they are, their words are not the ones that voters were choosing to adopt. The voters adopted the Constitution, not the Federalist Papers, and many of the states' voters weren't even exposed to the Federalist Papers.

The Federalist Papers themselves fall generally into three groups.

The first fourteen say nothing about the Constitution itself. They are an attempt to persuade the reader to the necessity of the thirteen States joining together with a central government "of some kind." There were many at the time who did not feel that a Union of all thirteen (if not more added later) States was a good idea. This group is making the case that the best idea for the future of the Americas is a single central government, rather than two or three Confederacies, as some wanted, or each State being fully sovereign and independent, as some also wanted. It would be possible for the Constitution to be rejected for its content, but for a majority to still want a Union of all. The object of this group was to persuade a majority to believe that a Union of all was the best course of action.

The second group, from XV to XXII, was a critique of the failures of the Articles of Confederation. The purpose here was to alert the voters to the dangers of doing nothing, as the current federal system was in danger of imminent collapse, which would expose them all to the hazards outlined in the first group of Papers.

The final group, from XXII to LXXXV discussed specific aspects of the proposed Constitution. Here one can often find the answers to the question of the purpose of particular provisions, what they wanted to avoid, what they wanted to happen, and other options which were considered as alternatives to the particular provision.

It is inarguable that the Federalist Papers are a valuable resource, and not merely for one who would learn more of the Constitution. However, my sole point is that for the purpose of understanding what it does, they are strictly "extra credit", and the person who reads the Constitution carefully need not feel intimidated by the "expert" who tries to use a reference to the Federalist Papers to persuade them that what they read does not mean what it clearly says.

In case I have not made myself clear, the Federalist Papers are worth reading, worthy of praise and respect, but are neither a substitute for reading the Constitution nor anything more than the comments of three, albeit eminently qualified, individuals on the subject of whether they should be adopted to form the government of the United States. If read as such, they have great value. If they are considered as anything more, they promise to confuse the reader.

# CHAPTER ELEVEN

## Comments On Alexis De Tocqueville

Another work often cited by those who present themselves as experts and authorities on the Constitution is the two volume work "Democracy in America" by Alexis de Tocqueville. As with the Federalist Papers, I do not mean to disparage Tocqueville in any way, but for the purpose of understanding the Constitution of the United States, his work is actually totally irrelevant. However, because he is cited so frequently by those who wish to be considered authorities on the Constitution, a somewhat deeper explanation of why I consider him to be irrelevant for that purpose is in order.

Alexis De Tocqueville was born in 1805. That fact alone should be enough for those who have read this book thus far to see why nothing in his book could have any impact or bearing on a document written almost twenty years before his birth. However, what he did have was a fairly unique perspective on how it was working for us at the time, given that he first came to America as an adult, and able to travel extensively on behalf of the French government, and look at our society, and did so a generation after the Constitution was adopted. From a point of view of examining American culture, society, and government, he has significant value. My point is that on the subject of the Constitution, knowledge of his book does not automatically grant anyone the status of authority or expert.

Without diminishing the value of such an objective view of how America worked a single generation after the establishment of the Constitution, it is, in the end, one point of view, but not the object viewed. While it is, like the Federalist Papers, a useful and brilliant work, it is a little more removed from the purpose of this book than even the Federalist Papers. The Federalist Papers were "about" the Constitution itself, and "Democracy in America" is more about the society formed under it. When examining our society, whether in the years preceding the Civil War, or today, the Constitution is sometimes a Cause and in other cases an Effect, and sometimes not even part of the equation at all. Tocqueville discussed other factors as well, including those geographic.

It also should be noted that "Democracy in America" has come in and out of fashion as a badge of authority over time, and has been quoted by people on all sides of the political spectrum. The observations and predictions it contains have been used to justify many opposing points of view on a variety of subjects, including economy, foreign policy, slavery, religion, and science. It has even been taken completely out of context by being made the subject of commemoration by the Library of Congress during the bicentennial of the French Revolution of 1789, which also occurred some 16 years before its author's birth.

Tocqueville's own limited point of view is actually exposed in his own introduction. He spends much time discussing the American "equality of social conditions", which seems odd considering his concerns expressed in later chapters about the existence of Slavery at the time. He traces recent French History from government by pure force, through several periods of increasing "democratization" of French society. One possible blind spot is revealed in his rhetorical question "Am I to believe that the Creator made man to leave him struggling endlessly with the intellectual wretchedness that surrounds us?" Tocqueville absolutely rejects that possibility, leading him to believe that the progression of History that he has observed has an absolute and Divinely Ordained endpoint, and that endpoint is some system of Harmony of Man, and that system is Democracy.

The biggest issue with this conclusion is that belief in there being an endpoint is to see History as a linear progression, which can only travel in one direction. Empirical evidence suggests that governmental systems are at least capable of moving toward more "intellectual wretchedness" as well as toward enlightenment, if not in altogether random directions as well. Progression can be cyclical or circular, and there may not be any endpoint at all.

If there is no final endpoint to societal evolution, then perhaps he is mistaken when he observes that "the people will seem peaceful not because they have abandoned the hope of better things but because they know they are well off." He doesn't seem to consider the possibility of unrest coming because the people may in fact be "well off" but told that they are not, by those who are unsatisfied with the status quo as it applies to themselves personally. He actually indicates his awareness of such motives, saying that despite a diminishing gap between rich and poor, such classes manage to find "fresh reasons for mutual hatred…for both of them equally, the concept of rights does not exist and power appears as the sole reason for action in the present and the only guarantee for the future."

Apparently enamored of America, he writes that "There is one country in the world where the great social revolution I speak of seems to have gradually reached its natural limits"; and yet, that country he was observing had not yet totally abolished Slavery, nor extended the right to vote to females.

However, Tocqueville himself was fully aware that his book was a single point of view. Despite his best efforts to be objective, and consider multiple sources in forming his impressions, he was aware enough of his limitations to predict that "nothing is easier than to criticize this book should anyone ever think of doing so." I would have to say that is demonstrably true, as I seem to have done so without any such intention.

And yet, it is not the book itself I mean to criticize here. I am merely criticizing it being used as an authoritative source on the Constitution itself. As a work observing societal impacts and considering possible future effects of the Constitution, it's not merely brilliant, it is unique. No one else with no specific agenda wrote such a book.

For someone who already knows the Constitution, it can offer a lot to help make the case to either follow the Constitution more closely, or to alter it to allow some effect that they consider desirable. In fact, both have been done at various times. However, it is no substitute for an understanding of the Constitution gained by first-hand reading of the Constitution itself.

# CHAPTER TWELVE

## A Few Cases

I promised early on that this wouldn't be a discussion of case law, and I still mean that. However, the fact is that many people, particularly lawyers, whose understanding of the Constitution is through case law.

As you've seen by reading it yourself, the Constitution created the USSC, and gave Congress the authority to establish lesser courts. That means that all of our courts are subordinate to the Constitution, and are given an implied power to "interpret" it, but they are not given any power to make any substantive changes in it. The only power to effect a real change in the Constitution is found in Article Five.

One of the first cases that is taught in Law Schools is Marbury vs. Madison. This is seen as the root case establishing their authority to decide what the Constitution contains. If you read the Constitution for yourself and formulate your own opinions, you'll eventually run into a lawyer who brings this case up to prove that you can't possibly know what you're talking about, so you need at least a working knowledge of the case.

The subject of the case was fairly straightforward. Mr. Marbury had been nominated to a post as Justice of the Peace by President John Adams. After his confirmation by the Senate, he was appointed, and the appropriate document of that commission was executed and delivered to the Secretary of State, John Marshall. John Marshall did not deliver it prior to Adams leaving office, and Jefferson directed his own Secretary of State James Madison to withhold it (along with several others). Marbury brought the suit requesting "mandamus", which is an Order of a court directing a government official to fulfill what is already their duty.

The Opinion of the Supreme Court examined the case as three separate questions. First, they determined whether or not Marbury was entitled to the Commission sought. After lengthy analysis, they determined that the appointment was effective when delivered to the Secretary of State by the President, and that everything else was a formality. Second, they considered whether or not there was a remedy for the failure to deliver. They concluded that there was, more or less because the presumption of the nature of Law that for every wrong there is a remedy.

The third question was whether or not the Court was empowered to grant that remedy.

This question was also subdivided into first determining the proper remedy, which they concluded was, in fact Mandamus. The final aspect of the Opinion dealt with whether or not the United States Supreme Court could issue a Writ of Mandamus to the Secretary of State to deliver the Commission in question. Despite having concluded that he should have done so, and that "somebody" should give such an order, they knew that it would weaken their own power to issue an order they had no power to enforce. They had to find a way to fold their hand without weakening their own authority by issuing an unenforceable order.

The Court examined the Constitution, and noted that their authority and jurisdiction derived from the Constitution, and not from Congress. The organization of Lesser Courts allowed Congress to divide Original jurisdiction among them as it saw fit, excepting those matters to which the Supreme Court was given Original jurisdiction. At the same time, where the Constitution granted the Supreme Court Appellate jurisdiction, that necessarily denied the Supreme Court Original jurisdiction. They could have one or the other in a particular matter, but not both.

The case was brought before the Supreme Court not as an Appeal from a lower court, because the act of Congress organizing the Judiciary gave Original jurisdiction to the Supreme Court. The decision was that this Congressional grant of authority contradicted the Constitution, and was therefore invalid. In other words, after page upon page of Opinion, they in the end declared that they had no jurisdiction in the first place.

Having no jurisdiction, they continued and firmly established themselves as the final authority to decide whether any other act of Congress exceeded the Constitutional limitations, and that "[i]t is emphatically the province and duty of the judicial department to say what the law is."

What that means is that they were able to declare what the result ought to be, and thereby censure Jefferson, without risking the embarrassment of issuing a ruling they had no power to enforce.

The net result of the decision was that President Jefferson got his way in the matter of the specific case, but the Supreme Court firmly established themselves as the last word on everything the government might do. It is somewhat ironic, given that Jefferson's unwillingness to complete the appointments was based in his desire to counter the Federalist's desire to load the Judiciary in their favor, the new positions having been created after his election and before his taking office. The decision did more than delivering the appointments would have.

As a final note, the reasoning for the last part of the decision was Constitutionally wrong anyway. They declined jurisdiction based on Article 3, Section 2 which states "In all the other Cases before mentioned, the supreme Court shall have appellate Jurisdiction, both as to Law and Fact", and determined that this clearly meant that Congress could not grant them Original jurisdiction. They overlooked the rest of the sentence, which reads "with such Exceptions, and under such Regulations as the Congress shall make."

As stated earlier, this is the usual start point for Law Schools teaching Constitutional Law. As far as cases go, there's actually a better one, that few lawyers seem to have read.

Little v. Barreme, 6 U.S. 2 Cranch 170 (1804)

The United States was at war with France in 1799. Congress passed a law intended to block sea borne commerce with France. As part of this Act, it authorized the President to authorize the Navy to stop private American vessels at sea, and if they were found to bound for a port controlled by France, to seize that ship, with half of the cargo becoming property of the United States, and the other half to those actually performing the seizure.

In December of 1799, the Flying Fish, a commercial vessel owned by a Prussian, and under the command of a native of Danish St. Thomas, was bound to St. Thomas from a French port in Hispaniola, carrying coffee. It was seized by the American Navy, and forfeiture was applied for in Boston district court.

That court ordered the vessel to be restored to the owners, because it was not, in fact, an American owned vessel, but refused to award any damages to the owners for the wrongful seizure. The issue of damages was appealed to the circuit court, which awarded damages.

The basis upon which damages were initially refused was that the court believed that Captain Little had sufficient Probable Cause to effect the seizure, as the order of the President made clear that the flag a ship flies is not determinative of the actual ownership of the vessel, or the nature of the cargo. However, the circuit court determined that there was, in fact, no probable cause, as the ship was not "bound to" a French port, as the underlying Act specified, but actually coming from one. The Act of Congress gave no authority to stop vessels outbound from French ports.

Captain Little was obeying Presidential orders, which contained the phrase "...you are to be vigilant that vessels or cargoes really American... bound to or from French ports do not escape you." However, the enabling legislation contained the clear limitation that only American ships bound TO French ports were subject to seizure, and a copy of the Act was provided to the ships' captains along with the orders that exceeded that authority.

There was no doubt that the Act was controlling for the question of the validity of the seizure. The ship and cargo were to be returned to the owners. The second question, which was the one appealed, was whether the Act or the Presidential Orders controlled for determining the Captain's personal liability for what was clearly an unlawful seizure.

The question is basically the same one that was raised after World War Two with what is now called "The Nuremburg Defense", that is, "I was following orders." The USSC in 1804 rejected that Defense, and placed personal responsibility for those acting under color of authority for the result of exceeding actual authority.

In the United States, federal government authority traces in every instance to the Constitution. The President did not have the power to expand what Congress had granted under its own Constitutional authority, so the orders were invalid, and obeyed by Captain Little at his own peril.

In this case, it was unnecessary to even examine the question of whether or not Congress had the authority to grant the power that it did, as the Presidential order exceeded that in any event. No authority was given to the Captains, so seizure of a vessel outbound from a French port was an unlawful act, responsibility for which descends upon the one who perpetrates it.

The reason why I think this would be a better starting point for law students is because it makes it clear that there are limits to what any branch or officer of the government may do, that these limits start with the Constitution, and apply to the Courts as well as the other branches. Marbury implies that the USSC has the power to declare what those limits are, even as applied to themselves, and that further investigation is moot once they declare what the Constitution says.

## The Dredd Scott Decision

This case, decided in 1857, could have been decided a number of ways. The facts were fairly simple. A slave, Dredd Scott, was taken from Missouri, which recognized Slavery, into Illinois, which did not. Scott's suit was that this made him Free.

The question came down to whether Missouri Law controlled or Illinois. Problematic was that Illinois' prohibition on Slavery derived from an act of Congress when the Louisiana Purchase was made. In reaching their decision, it was necessary that the Court void that particular Act (which Marbury made possible). They could not void the state Law per se, as Illinois was still considered a sovereign. However, the root of that state law was a federal act, which they were able to reach, saying "the act of Congress which prohibited a citizen from holding and owning property of this kind in the territory of the United States north of the line therein mentioned, is not warranted by the Constitution, and is therefore void; and that neither Dred Scott himself, nor any of his family, were made free by being carried into this territory." In other words, they said Congress had overreached by deciding the issue of Slavery in Illinois as a condition of its Statehood, having no such authority under the Constitution to do so.

However, notice that by their having started with the assumption that it was a Property matter, the result was a foregone conclusion. Had they started with the assumption that it was a question of individual rights, the result would have been quite different, as they themselves acknowledged by saying that viewing people of African descent as citizens "...would give to persons of the negro race, who were recognized as citizens in any one State of the Union, the right to enter every other State whenever they pleased... to go where they pleased at every hour of the day or night without molestation, unless they committed some violation of law for which a white man would be punished; and it would give them the full liberty of speech in public and in private upon all subjects upon which its own citizens might speak; to hold public meetings upon political affairs, and to keep and carry arms wherever they went." In other words, had they not decided the case as a matter of Property Law, the result would have likely ended Slavery in the United States immediately.

It would be interesting to see what more learned Historians than I believe what would have happened in the United States had they done so. If such a decision did end the institution of Slavery right then, it might or might not have triggered the Secession three years earlier. If it had, the question is what the reaction of President Buchanan would have been. It is possible that the Union have ultimately been re-established peacefully but without Slavery, and without the destruction of the South in the War and its aftermath, The Reconstruction. It's on my list of "unwritten books I'd like to read."

The point here is that the USSC doesn't always get it right. You can't simply take anyone's word for what the Constitution says, not even the USSC, and particularly not what other people tell you the USSC said. You have to read it and think for yourself.

## Roe v. Wade

A lot has been written about this case, but there are aspects to it that many people overlook entirely.

First of all, this case was pretty much decided in the oral argument phase, when one of the Justices asked the attorney presenting the case for the State of Texas whether Texas asserted any interest in the life of the unborn fetus. When the answer was negative, it was over. The deciding factor wasn't the mother's Constitutional "right to privacy", what made that decisive was that there were no other rights to weigh those against.

Whether an abortion law classifies itself as a Homicide or not, that's the reality of what such a law must be. If the fetus is not a "person" under the law, then such a law has little justification. Without the fetus being a "person", then the only rights in the equation are those of the mother. If the state doesn't assert an interest in the unborn, then it is not a "person", and it doesn't matter how much or how little the rights of the mother, they are superior to that which does not legally exist.

The case was specifically about Texas laws banning abortion, and generally about those of other states. The Texas laws in question enhanced the punishment for doing so without the consent of the mother, so they could serve no other purpose than to protect the fetus. If Texas asserted no interest in the fetus, there's no explanation for why the law was written in the first place.

In other words, the attorney for Texas didn't just drop the

ball, he carried to his own end zone just prior to the fumble.

Had Texas asserted such an interest, the laws would be among all others in the category of Homicide, which has always been the province of the States, and the USSC would have been without jurisdiction. Texas would be defining a class of "victim", which every criminal law must do, and states are well within their sovereign powers to draft as they see fit.

The question in creating such legislation is when a fetus might obtain rights that the State chooses to and may protect. Certainly the mother has a right to prevent the fetus from ever existing, but at some point, those rights are superseded by those of the offspring, and the entire issue is when that point is reached. Obviously that happens at some point; to ignore this question would be to say that a mother has the eternal right to end the life of her offspring. Viewed logically, the line that such laws draw must necessarily be drawn "somewhere", and failure to assert a state interest in the fetus allowed the decision to be made without acknowledging that the line exists.

Even having evaded the real issue in this way, the USSC still had to find a Constitutional basis for the decision. They ultimately decided to do so based on a "right to privacy."

Where the USSC found this right was "emanating" from a "penumbra" of rights. In other words, it isn't explicitly there, but they decided that the concept of privacy was underneath all of the other rights. Again, Marbury says that they can do that, but that doesn't mean they were not in error. They were in error, but not simply because the word "privacy" is absent in the Constitution.

It was an error because it is clear that the right of privacy, even assuming it exists, is not absolute. The entire 4th Amendment deals with when and how a person's privacy, in the form of their "papers and persons" may be violated. In other words, the "right to privacy" can exist, but not necessarily be violated by a prohibition on abortion. There needed to be some kind of balancing of the rights of the fetus, which, oral argument notwithstanding, were asserted by the very existence of the Texas law. Relieved of the requirement to consider those, the mother's privacy was unopposed.

It was also an error because even if a right to privacy exists, there's no need to find it in some "penumbra" that only the elite few can even see. It would be covered by the Ninth Amendment, which you can look at for yourself in Appendix 5.

## Bush vs Gore

I'm not willing to spend a lot of time on these cases at this point. Perhaps I will change my mind prior to this book going to print, but at the moment, I simply don't feel inclined to do so.

Instead, I'm going to acknowledge that "conventional wisdom" is that the USSC basically changed the outcome of the election in Florida, and hence nationwide, effectively "selecting" or "appointing" George W. Bush.

If you've made it this far in this book, then you shouldn't be taking anyone else's word for what these cases say, either, so you should look them up for yourself.

If you will do a web search on "bush v. gore", you will find four cases, two from the Florida Supreme Court, and two from the US Supreme Court. Sequentially, the FSC made a ruling, that was appealed to the USSC, which issued a ruling, and the FSC made a new ruling, which was also appealed to the USSC. Read the four in sequence for yourself, and you'll see the truth of what really happened. Do not believe anyone else, not even myself. The Truth is too important to entrust to others.

# NOW WHAT

## "To Ourselves And Posterity"

Well, that greatly depends on whether or not you see any significant difference between our federal government as it exists today and the Constitution. I can't see how anyone could read it and see all the various things the government is involved in and come to any other conclusion, but I suppose there are those that think everything is according to the Constitution.

Even assuming you recognize the disparity, it is a threshold question whether you see that as a problem. As you know from the overview of History provided, the American Revolution wasn't fought over any specific issue such as Taxation. The Revolution was fought against the idea of being subject to a government that had no limitation on its authority. If our current government does not stay within the limitations of the Constitution, we're in the same situation, even if we currently feel somewhat comfortable with it. Of course, if we are comfortable with it now, we should remember that the people who started fighting the Revolution in 1776 were also comfortable in 1774.

Let me be clear that I do not advocate any course of action that involves violence or even breaking the laws. While our Founding Fathers were cognizant that such a point could be reached, and that violence was justifiable when it is reached, we are by no means anywhere near that point. We still have the Constitution, and our elected officials still swear an oath to uphold it. We didn't have that in 1776. This situation can be resolved peacefully. Our situation was arrived at with the consent, whether active or passive, of the majority of Americans. To even consider resorting to violence means at this point is to deny our own responsibility for our situation.

That is the first step. We have to acknowledge our own responsibility for the situation, and that changing anything is also our responsibility. Wisdom unaccompanied by action is no better than ignorance. We have to recognize that it is up to us to demand that it change.

What I should hope you realize is that the government is acting beyond the Constitution, and recognize this in itself as a problem, which demands correction. Even if most people were to agree on that much, we still have one great question to answer before we can make any kind of plan to move forward:

Where the government is exceeding the Constitution, do we want them to stop, or do we want to give them authority to do what they are doing already?

For example, I think that there's simply no question that there's no federal authority to be involved in the War on Drugs. Taking that as a premise, the question is whether or not we as a nation approve of it, and if we do, we should properly grant them this authority through a Constitutional Amendment. The one thing we should not do is continue to ignore the situation, as it will only encourage moving further and further away from recognizing the limitations.

That's what we need to do with every single area where the federal government has involved itself. We need to either demand that the excesses stop, or grant them the authority to continue. To continue to ignore the situation as a "comfortable compromise" simply makes the Constitution functionally irrelevant, which means our government has no limitations.

Take note, however, that this choice is not an "all or nothing." There's no reason we can't expand the federal authority to allow them to do "some" of the things they are doing that it doesn't permit, and at the same time demand that other things cease. The decision is, or should be, up to ourselves as a body, the People, and we can pick and choose.

If this is to become any kind of "movement", then our

first objective needs to be to change the debate in our own local areas. When we have an opportunity to speak with or ask questions of candidates for federal office, we need to speak in terms of the Constitution. If a candidate says they plan to make something a priority, ask them where in the Constitution they would get the authority to do that. We need to make the Constitution the focus of all political debate.

Speaking for myself, we need to be wary of turning this over to either or both of the existing political parties, nor can we allow it to be the exclusive domain of any other party. In the first place, regarding political parties as the guardians of our Constitution is precisely how we got where we are, and moreover, nationwide political parties are one of the dangers that the authors of the Constitution sought to protect us from. In the final analysis, we aren't primarily seeking any changes to our government, other than to have it conform itself to the Constitution. We don't need a political party for that, we just need to be aware of the excesses, and vote for people that are also aware, and who we at least believe to be willing to abide by the Constitution.

That's our responsibility as the People who created it. If the federal government is no longer abiding by it, then it is our responsibility to call them on it, and demand they stay within its boundaries. History shows that they otherwise will not, and that we cannot rely upon political parties to enforce it on our behalf.

To make that happen, you need to do what you can to promote the very premise of this book. You need to talk to those around you, and persuade them to read the Constitution as well. It needs to be familiar to everyone, and reject the concept of accepting anyone as an "expert" on the subject, and certainly demand that the "experts" support their assertions with Constitutional references. One person alone doesn't make as much noise as two.

All of that is possible to do as individuals. We need to

start by doing those as individuals, and only then will we find ourselves in groups of like-minded people, and able to work together on specific more active measures, by which I still do not mean "violence." By "active measures", I mean demanding adherence to the Constitution by your votes and political support, and also supporting change where necessary.

If we can first get to the point where the desire to hold the government within the Constitution becomes a "mainstream" point of view, only then can we hope to make any further changes that we might want to make. The first step is not to redraft the Constitution or make numerous amendments, it is to cause compliance with it as it exists now. If the problem is extra-Constitutional activity, it is pointless to make any changes to it for any reason. The first step is enforcement of what we already have.

Once we manage that, then we could start to discuss specific Amendments that might be proposed to correct problems that the Constitution as it exists might be causing.

For example, the Sixteenth Amendment permits the federal government to levy a tax on income. Our founders knew this to be a practice harmful to a country's economy at any level, and perhaps our century of experience with it would persuade us that their fears are unfounded. Perhaps we don't wish to do away with Income tax completely. However, I think we should consider placing some form of absolute ceiling on the rates that can be levied. As written, they are not even limited to the theoretical and logical limit of 100%. I think that could be clarified to preclude at least a rate that all would agree is "excessive."

I believe that one of the biggest problems we have in this country is our lack of political choices. In this current election year 2008, both major parties agree that the government should have some role in Health Care and protection of the Environment. I'm unable to find any such authority for either in the Constitution, but that's not the point right now. The fact is that there are other parties, but little attention is paid to them. Voters pay little attention because the media pays little attention, and the media pays little attention because their chances of actually winning are slim. Their chances of winning are significantly impacted by various State legislation, and sometimes State Constitutions which guarantee significant advantages to the two major parties. If the idea of conforming to the Constitution became an idea most of us could share, the problems caused by granting specific parties legally protected status within the government would be more apparent to everyone.

Alexander Hamilton and George Washington warned us several times about the dangers of "factions." That's what political parties are. We have not only ignored the warnings, we have allowed the factions to gain protected status under the laws. Most Republicans don't like the ideas of Democrats and vice-versa. I cannot see how either can argue that while the other is wrong, that any other "third party" must be even more wrong. Looking at what passes for political discourse now, I can't imagine what it would take to be more wrong than each portrays the other, each claims the other to be "Nazis", and of "stealing" elections, among other things. How could the Greens or the Libertarians possibly be worse than that? Why would the two major parties object to opening the process to other ideas?

What we need to do about that situation would ideally be to root out any such preferences to any party on a state-by-state basis, but this is not likely to ever be achieved. An arguably difficult solution, but the only one that is likely to work, would be an Amendment declaring any such preference, whether in state or federal laws or in a state Constitution to be utterly void.

Possibly the hardest thing we need to learn to do is to abandon the tendency to vote for the least offensive alternative. By choosing the candidate that will do less harm, we are accepting the outcome as being harmful. We have to demand and give our support to the best possible outcome, and vote as if we knew we would be casting the deciding vote. To do otherwise is not Democracy anyway.

To enforce the Constitution, we can use a variety of means. Most of these involve the federal ballot box. We must demand that those whom we elect understand and agree to abide by the Constitution, and they must certainly be aware that we know what it says and we are watching.

We have to stop trusting the government to govern itself, and stop relying on one or both parties to govern the government. We have to do that.

It all starts by us reading the Constitution, and not allowing anyone else to convince us that we aren't competent to understand what we read, and that becoming an everyday topic among We the People.

Ourselves and Posterity                    93

*Secure the Blessings of Liberty*

# APPENDICES

*Secure the Blessings of Liberty*

# APPENDIX 1

## The Articles of Association

### October 20, 1774

We, his majesty's most loyal subjects, the delegates of the several colonies of New-Hampshire, Massachusetts-Bay, Rhode-Island, Connecticut, New-York, New-Jersey, Pennsylvania, the three lower counties of Newcastle, Kent and Sussex on Delaware, Maryland, Virginia, North-Carolina, and South-Carolina, deputed to represent them in a continental Congress, held in the city of Philadelphia, on the 5th day of September, 1774, avowing our allegiance to his majesty, our affection and regard for our fellow-subjects in Great-Britain and elsewhere, affected with the deepest anxiety, and most alarming apprehensions, at those grievances and distresses, with which his Majesty's American subjects are oppressed; and having taken under our most serious deliberation, the state of the whole continent, find, that the present unhappy situation of our affairs is occasioned by a ruinous system of colony administration, adopted by the British ministry about the year 1763, evidently calculated for enslaving these colonies, and, with them, the British Empire. In prosecution of which system, various acts of parliament have been passed, for raising a revenue in America, for depriving the American subjects, in many instances, of the constitutional trial by jury, exposing their lives to danger, by directing a new and illegal trial beyond the seas, for crimes alleged to have been committed in America: And in prosecution of the same system, several late, cruel, and oppressive acts have been passed, respecting the town of Boston and the Massachusetts-Bay, and also an act for extending the province of Quebec, so as to border on the western frontiers of these colonies, establishing an arbitrary government therein, and discouraging the settlement of British subjects in that wide extended country; thus, by the influence of civil principles and ancient prejudices, to dispose the inhabitants to act with hostility against the free Protestant colonies, whenever a wicked ministry shall chuse so to direct them.

To obtain redress of these grievances, which threaten destruction to the lives liberty, and property of his majesty's subjects, in North-America, we are of opinion, that a non-importation, non-consumption, and non-exportation agreement, faithfully adhered to, will prove the most speedy, effectual, and peaceable measure: And, therefore, we do, for ourselves, and the inhabitants of the several colonies, whom we represent, firmly agree and associate, under the sacred ties of virtue, honour and love of our country, as follows:

1. That from and after the first day of

December next, we will not import, into British America, from Great-Britain or Ireland, any goods, wares, or merchandise whatsoever, or from any other place, any such goods, wares, or merchandise, as shall have been exported from Great-Britain or Ireland; nor will we, after that day, import any East-India tea from any part of the world; nor any molasses, syrups, paneles, coffee, or pimento, from the British plantations or from Dominica; nor wines from Madeira, or the Western Islands; nor foreign indigo.

2. We will neither import nor purchase, any slave imported after the first day of December next; after which time, we will wholly discontinue the slave trade, and will neither be concerned in it ourselves, nor will we hire our vessels, nor sell our commodities or manufactures to those who are concerned in it.

3. As a non-consumption agreement, strictly adhered to, will be an effectual security for the observation of the non-importation, we, as above, solemnly agree and associate, that from this day, we will not purchase or use any tea, imported on account of the East-India company, or any on which a duty hath been or shall be paid; and from and after the first day of March next, we will not purchase or use any East-India tea whatever; nor will we, nor shall any person for or under us, purchase or use

any of those goods, wares, or merchandise, we have agreed not to import, which we shall know, or have cause to suspect, were imported after the first day of December, except such as come under the rules and directions of the tenth article hereafter mentioned.

4. The earnest desire we have not to injure our fellow-subjects in Great-Britain, Ireland, or the West-Indies, induces us to suspend a non-exportation, until the tenth day of September, 1775; at which time, if the said acts and parts of acts of the British parliament herein after mentioned, are not repealed, we will not directly or indirectly, export any merchandise or commodity whatsoever to Great-Britain, Ireland, or the West-Indies, except rice to Europe.

5. Such as are merchants, and use the British and Irish trade, will give orders, as soon as possible, to their factors, agents and correspondents, in Great-Britain and Ireland, not to ship any goods to them, on any pretence whatsoever, as they cannot be received in America; and if any merchant, residing in Great-Britain or Ireland, shall directly or indirectly ship any goods, wares or merchandize, for America, in order to break the said non-importation agreement, or in any manner contravene the same, on such unworthy conduct being well attested, it ought to

be made public; and, on the same being so done, we will not, from thenceforth, have any commercial connexion with such merchant.

6. That such as are owners of vessels will give positive orders to their captains, or masters, not to receive on board their vessels any goods prohibited by the said non-importation agreement, on pain of immediate dismission from their service.

7. We will use our utmost endeavours to improve the breed of sheep, and increase their number to the greatest extent; and to that end, we will kill them as seldom as may be, especially those of the most profitable kind; nor will we export any to the West-Indies or elsewhere; and those of us, who are or may become overstocked with, or can conveniently spare any sheep, will dispose of them to our neighbors, especially to the poorer sort, on moderate terms.

8. We will, in our several stations, encourage frugality, economy, and industry, and promote agriculture, arts and the manufactures of this country, especially that of wool; and will discountenance and discourage every species of extravagance and dissipation, especially all horse-racing, and all kinds of games, cock fighting, exhibitions of shews, plays, and other expensive diversions and entertainments;

and on the death of any relation or friend, none of us, or any of our families will go into any further mourning-dress, than a black crepe or ribbon on the arm or hat, for gentlemen, and a black ribbon and necklace for ladies, and we will discontinue the giving of gloves and scarves at funerals.

9. Such as are venders of goods or merchandize will not take advantage of the scarcity of goods, that may be occasioned by this association, but will sell the same at the rates we have been respectively accustomed to do, for twelve months last past. -And if any vender of goods or merchandise shall sell such goods on higher terms, or shall, in any manner, or by any device whatsoever, violate or depart from this agreement, no person ought, nor will any of us deal with any such person, or his or her factor or agent, at any time thereafter, for any commodity whatever.

10. In case any merchant, trader, or other person, shall import any goods or merchandize, after the first day of December, and before the first day of February next, the same ought forthwith, at the election of the owner, to be either re-shipped or delivered up to the committee of the country or town, wherein they shall be imported, to be stored at the risque of the importer, until the non-importation agreement shall cease, or be sold under the direction of the committee aforesaid; and in the last-

mentioned case, the owner or owners of such goods shall be reimbursed out of the sales, the first cost and charges, the profit, if any, to be applied towards relieving and employing such poor inhabitants of the town of Boston, as are immediate sufferers by the Boston port-bill; and a particular account of all goods so returned, stored, or sold, to be inserted in the public papers; and if any goods or merchandises shall be imported after the said first day of February, the same ought forthwith to be sent back again, without breaking any of the packages thereof.

*11.* That a committee be chosen in every county, city, and town, by those who are qualified to vote for representatives in the legislature, whose business it shall be attentively to observe the conduct of all persons touching this association; and when it shall be made to appear, to the satisfaction of a majority of any such committee, that any person within the limits of their appointment has violated this association, that such majority do forthwith cause the truth of the case to be published in the gazette; to the end, that all such foes to the rights of British-America may be publicly known, and universally contemned as the enemies of American liberty; and thenceforth we respectively will break off all dealings with him or her.

*12.* That the committee of correspondence,

in the respective colonies, do frequently inspect the entries of their customhouses, and inform each other, from time to time, of the true state thereof, and of every other material circumstance that may occur relative to this association.

13. That all manufactures of this country be sold at reasonable prices, so- that no undue advantage be taken of a future scarcity of goods.

14. And we do further agree and resolve that we will have no trade, commerce, dealings or intercourse whatsoever, with any colony or province, in North-America, which shall not accede to, or which shall hereafter violate this association, but will hold them as unworthy of the rights of freemen, and as inimical to the liberties of their country.

And we do solemnly bind ourselves and our constituents, under the ties aforesaid, to adhere to this association, until such parts of the several acts of parliament passed since the close of the last war, as impose or continue duties on tea, wine, molasses, syrups paneles, coffee, sugar, pimento, indigo, foreign paper, glass, and painters' colours, imported into America, and extend the powers of the admiralty courts beyond their ancient limits, deprive the American subject of trial by jury, authorize the judge's certificate to indemnify the prosecutor from damages, that he might otherwise be liable to from a trial by his peers, require oppressive security from a claimant of ships or goods seized, before he shall be allowed to defend his property, are repealed.-And until that part of the act of the 12 G. 3. ch. 24, entitled "An act for the better securing his majesty's dock-yards magazines, ships, ammunition, and stores," by which any persons charged with committing any of the offenses therein described, in America, may be tried in any shire or county within the realm, is repealed-and until the four acts, passed the last session of parliament, viz. that for stopping the port and blocking up the harbour of Boston-that for altering the charter and government of the Massachusetts-Bay-and that which is entitled "An act for the better administration of justice, &c."-and that "for extending the limits of Quebec, &c." are repealed. And we recommend it to the provincial conventions, and to the committees in the respective colonies, to establish such farther regulations as they may think proper, for carrying into execution this association.

The foregoing association being determined upon by the Congress, was ordered to be subscribed by the several members thereof; and thereupon, we have hereunto set our respective names accordingly.

IN CONGRESS, PHILADELPHIA, October 20, 1774.

PEYTON RANDOLPH, President.

- **New Hampshire**
- Jno. Sullivan
- Nathel. Folsom
- **Massachusetts Bay**
- Thomas Cushing
- Saml. Adams
- John Adams
- Robt.Treat Paine
- **Rhode Island**
- Step. Hopkins
- Sam: Ward
- **Connecticut**
- Elipht Dyer
- Roger Sherman
- Silas Deane
- **New York**
- Isaac Low
- John Alsop
- John Jay
- Jas. Duane
- Phil. Livingston

- Wm. Floyd
- Henry Wisner
- S: Boerum
- **New Jersey**
- J. Kinsey
- Wil: Livingston
- Stepn. Crane
- Richd. Smith
- John De Hart
- **Pennsylvania**
- Jos. Galloway
- John Dickinson
- Cha Humphreys
- Thomas Mifflin
- E. Biddle
- John Morton
- Geo: Ross
- **The Lower Counties New Castle**
- Cæsar Rodney
- Tho. M: Kean
- Geo: Read
- **Maryland**

- Mat Tilghman

- Ths. Johnson Junr.

- Wm. Paca

- Samuel Chase

# APPENDIX 2

## The Declaration of Independence of the Thirteen Colonies

In CONGRESS, July 4, 1776

**The unanimous Declaration of the thirteen united States of America,**

When in the Course of human events, it becomes necessary for one people to dissolve the political bands which have connected them with another, and to assume among the powers of the earth, the separate and equal station to which the Laws of Nature and of Nature's God entitle them, a decent respect to the opinions of mankind requires that they should declare the causes which impel them to the separation.

We hold these truths to be self-evident, that all men are created equal, that they are endowed by their Creator with certain unalienable Rights, that among these are Life, Liberty and the pursuit of Happiness. --That to secure these rights, Governments are instituted among Men, deriving their just powers from the consent of the governed, --That whenever any Form of Government becomes destructive of these ends, it is the Right of the People to alter or to abolish it, and to institute new Government, laying its foundation on such principles and organizing its powers in such form, as to them shall seem most likely to effect their Safety and Happiness. Prudence, indeed, will dictate that Governments long established should not be changed for light and transient causes; and accordingly all experience hath shewn, that mankind are more disposed to suffer, while evils are sufferable, than to right themselves by abolishing the forms to which they are accustomed. But when a long train of abuses and usurpations, pursuing invariably the same Object evinces a design to reduce them under absolute Despotism, it is their right, it is their duty, to throw off such Government, and to provide new Guards for their future security. —Such has been the patient sufferance of these Colonies; and such is now the necessity which constrains them to alter their former Systems of Government. The history of the present King of Great Britain [George III] is a history of repeated injuries and usurpations, all having in direct object the establishment of an absolute Tyranny over these States. To prove this, let Facts be submitted to a candid world.

He has refused his Assent to Laws, the most wholesome and necessary for the public good.

He has forbidden his Governors to pass Laws of immediate and pressing importance, unless suspended in their operation till his Assent should be obtained; and when so suspended, he has utterly neglected to attend to them.

He has refused to pass other Laws for the accommodation of large districts of people, unless those people would relinquish the right of Representation in the Legislature, a right inestimable to them and formidable to tyrants only.

He has called together legislative bodies at places unusual, uncomfortable, and distant from the depository of their public Records, for the sole purpose of fatiguing them into compliance with his measures.

He has dissolved Representative Houses repeatedly, for opposing with manly firmness his invasions on the rights of the people.

He has refused for a long time, after such dissolutions, to cause others to be elected; whereby the Legislative powers, incapable of Annihilation, have returned to the People at large for their exercise; the State remaining in the mean time exposed to all the dangers of invasion from without, and convulsions within.

He has endeavoured to prevent the population of these States; for that purpose obstructing the Laws for Naturalization of Foreigners; refusing to pass others to encourage their migrations hither, and raising the conditions of new Appropriations of Lands. He has obstructed the Administration of Justice, by refusing his Assent to Laws for establishing Judiciary powers.

He has made Judges dependent on his Will alone, for the tenure of their offices, and the amount and payment of their salaries.

He has erected a multitude of New Offices, and sent hither swarms of Officers to harass our people, and eat out their substance.

He has kept among us, in times of peace, Standing Armies without the consent of our legislatures.

He has affected to render the Military independent of and superior to the Civil power.

He has combined with others to subject us to a jurisdiction foreign to our constitution and unacknowledged by our laws; giving his Assent to their Acts of pretended Legislation:

For Quartering large bodies of armed troops among us:

For protecting them, by a mock Trial, from punishment for any Murders which they should commit on the Inhabitants of these States:

For cutting off our Trade with all parts of the world:

For imposing Taxes on us without our Consent:

For depriving us, in many cases, of the benefits of Trial by Jury:

For transporting us beyond Seas to be tried for pretended offences:

For abolishing the free System of English Laws in a neighboring Province, establishing therein an Arbitrary government, and enlarging its Boundaries so as to render it at once an example and fit instrument for introducing the same absolute rule into these Colonies:

For taking away our Charters, abolishing our most valuable Laws, and altering fundamentally the Forms of our Governments:

For suspending our own Legislatures, and declaring themselves invested with power to legislate for us in all cases whatsoever.

He has abdicated Government here, by declaring us out of his Protection and waging War against us.

He has plundered our seas, ravaged our Coasts, burnt our towns, and destroyed the lives of our people.

He is at this time transporting large Armies of foreign Mercenaries to compleat the works of death, desolation and tyranny, already begun with circumstances of Cruelty and perfidy scarcely paralleled in the most barbarous ages, and totally unworthy the Head of a civilized nation.

He has constrained our fellow Citizens taken Captive on the high Seas to bear Arms against their Country, to become the executioners of their friends and Brethren, or to fall themselves by their Hands.

He has excited domestic insurrections amongst us, and has endeavoured to bring on the inhabitants of our frontiers, the merciless Indian Savages, whose known rule of warfare, is an undistinguished destruction of all ages, sexes and conditions.

In every stage of these Oppressions We have Petitioned for Redress in the most humble terms: Our repeated Petitions have been answered only by repeated injury. A Prince whose character is thus marked by every act which may define a Tyrant, is unfit to be the ruler of a free people.

Nor have We been wanting in attentions to our British brethren. We have warned them from time to time of attempts by their legislature to extend an unwarrantable jurisdiction over us. We have reminded them of the circumstances of our emigration and settlement here. We have appealed to their native justice and magnanimity, and we have conjured them by the ties of our common kindred to disavow these usurpations, which, would inevitably interrupt our connections and correspondence. They too have been deaf to the voice of justice and of consanguinity. We must, therefore, acquiesce in the necessity, which denounces our Separation, and hold them, as we hold the rest of mankind, Enemies in War, in Peace Friends.

We, therefore, the Representatives of the united States of America, in General Congress, Assembled, appealing to the Supreme Judge of the world for the rectitude of our intentions, do, in the Name, and by the Authority of the good People of these Colonies, solemnly publish and declare, That these United Colonies are, and of Right ought to be Free and Independent States; that they are Absolved from all Allegiance to the British Crown, and that all political connection between them and the State of Great Britain, is and ought to be totally dissolved; and that as Free and Independent States, they have full Power to levy War, conclude Peace, contract Alliances, establish Commerce, and to do all other Acts and Things which Independent States may of right do. And for the support of this Declaration, with a firm reliance on the protection of divine Providence, we mutually pledge to each other our Lives, our Fortunes and our sacred Honor.

*The signers of the Declaration represented the new states as follows:*

## New Hampshire

Josiah Bartlett, William Whipple, Matthew Thornton

## Massachusetts

John Hancock, Samuel Adams, John Adams, Robert Treat Paine, Elbridge Gerry

## Rhode Island

Stephen Hopkins, William Ellery

## Connecticut

Roger Sherman, Samuel Huntington, William Williams, Oliver Wolcott

## New York

William Floyd, Philip Livingston, Francis Lewis, Lewis Morris

## New Jersey

Richard Stockton, John Witherspoon, Francis Hopkinson, John Hart, Abraham Clark

## Pennsylvania

Robert Morris, Benjamin Rush, Benjamin Franklin, John Morton, George Clymer, James Smith, George Taylor, James Wilson, George Ross

## Delaware

Caesar Rodney, George Read, Thomas McKean

## Maryland

Samuel Chase, William Paca, Thomas Stone, Charles Carroll of Carrollton

## Virginia

George Wythe, Richard Henry Lee, Thomas Jefferson, Benjamin Harrison, Thomas Nelson, Jr., Francis Lightfoot Lee, Carter Braxton

## North Carolina

William Hooper, Joseph Hewes, John Penn

## South Carolina

Edward Rutledge, Thomas Heyward, Jr., Thomas Lynch, Jr., Arthur Middleton

## Georgia

Button Gwinnett, Lyman Hall, George Walton

*Secure the Blessings of Liberty*

# APPENDIX 3

## The Articles of Confederation

Agreed to by Congress November 15, 1777; ratified and in force, March 1, 1781.

### Preamble

To all to whom these Presents shall come, we the undersigned Delegates of the States affixed to our Names send greeting.

Articles of Confederation and perpetual Union between the States of New Hampshire, Massachusetts bay, Rhode Island and Providence Plantations, Connecticut, New York, New Jersey, Pennsylvania, Delaware, Maryland, Virginia, North Carolina, South Carolina and Georgia.

Article I. The Stile of this Confederacy shall be "The United States of America."

Article II. Each state retains its sovereignty, freedom, and independence, and every power, jurisdiction, and right, which is not by this Confederation expressly delegated to the United States, in Congress assembled.

Article III. The said States hereby severally enter into a firm league of friendship with each other, for their common defense, the security of their liberties, and their mutual and general welfare, binding themselves to assist each other, against all force offered to, or attacks made upon them, or any of them, on account of religion, sovereignty, trade, or any other pretense whatever.

Article IV. The better to secure and perpetuate mutual friendship and intercourse among the people of the different States in this Union, the free inhabitants of each of these States, paupers, vagabonds, and fugitives from justice excepted, shall be entitled to all privileges and immunities of free citizens in the several States; and the people of each State shall free ingress and regress to and from any other State, and shall enjoy therein all the privileges of trade and commerce, subject to the same duties, impositions, and restrictions as the inhabitants thereof respectively, provided that such restrictions shall not extend so far as to prevent the removal of property imported into any State, to any other State, of which the owner is an inhabitant; provided also that no imposition, duties or restriction shall be laid by any State, on the property of the United States, or either of them.

If any person guilty of, or charged with, treason, felony, or other high misdemeanor in any State, shall flee from justice, and be found in any of the United States, he shall, upon demand of the Governor or executive power of the State from which he fled, be delivered up and removed to the State having jurisdiction of his offense.

Full faith and credit shall be given in each of these States to the records, acts, and judicial proceedings of the courts and magistrates of every other State.

Article V. For the most convenient management of the general interests of the United States, delegates shall be annually appointed in such manner as the legislatures of each State shall direct, to meet in Congress on the first Monday in November, in every year, with a power reserved to each State to recall its delegates, or any of them, at any time within the year, and to send others in their stead for the remainder of the year.

No State shall be represented in Congress by less than two, nor more than seven members; and no person shall be capable of being a delegate for more than three years in any term of six years; nor shall any person, being a delegate, be capable of holding any office under the United States, for which he, or another for his benefit, receives any salary, fees or emolument of any kind.

Each State shall maintain its own delegates in a meeting of the States, and while they act as members of the committee of the States.

In determining questions in the United States in Congress assembled, each State shall have one vote.

Freedom of speech and debate in Congress shall not be impeached or questioned in any court or place out of Congress, and the members of Congress shall be protected in their persons from arrests or imprisonments, during the time of their going to and from, and attendance on Congress, except for treason, felony, or breach of the peace.

Article VI. No State, without the consent of the United States in Congress assembled, shall send any embassy to, or receive any embassy from, or enter into any conference, agreement, alliance or treaty with any King, Prince or State; nor shall any person holding any office of profit or trust under the United States, or any of them, accept any present, emolument, office or title of any kind whatever from any King, Prince or foreign State; nor shall the United States in Congress assembled, or any of them, grant any title of nobility.

No two or more States shall enter into any treaty, confederation or alliance whatever between them, without the consent of the United States in Congress assembled, specifying accurately the purposes for which the same is to be entered into, and how long it shall continue.

No State shall lay any imposts or duties, which may interfere with any stipulations in treaties, entered into by the United States in Congress assembled, with any King, Prince or State, in pursuance of any treaties already proposed by Congress, to the courts of France and Spain.

No vessel of war shall be kept up in time of peace by any State, except such number only, as shall be deemed necessary by the United States in Congress assembled, for the defense of such State, or its trade; nor shall any body of forces be kept up by any State in time of peace, except such number only, as in the judgement of the United States in Congress assembled, shall be deemed requisite to garrison the forts necessary for the defense of such State; but every State shall always keep up a well-regulated and disciplined militia, sufficiently armed and accoutered, and shall provide and constantly have ready for use, in public stores, a due number of filed pieces and tents, and a proper quantity of arms, ammunition and camp equipage.

No State shall engage in any war without the consent of the United States in Congress assembled, unless such State be actually invaded by enemies, or shall have received certain advice of a resolution being formed by some nation of Indians to invade such State, and the danger is so imminent as not to admit of a delay till the United States in Congress assembled can be consulted; nor shall any State grant commissions to any ships or vessels of war, nor letters of marque or reprisal, except it be after a declaration of war by the United States in Congress assembled, and then only against the Kingdom or State and the subjects thereof, against which war has been so declared, and under such regulations as shall be established by the United States in Congress assembled, unless such State be infested by pirates, in which case vessels of war may be fitted out for that occasion, and kept so long as the danger shall continue, or until the United States in Congress assembled shall determine otherwise.

Article VII. When land forces are raised by any State for the common defense, all officers of or under the rank of colonel, shall be appointed by the legislature of each State respectively, by whom such forces shall be raised, or in such manner as such State shall direct, and all vacancies shall be filled up by the State which first made the appointment.

Article VIII. All charges of war, and all other expenses that shall be incurred for the common defense or general welfare, and allowed by the United States in Congress assembled, shall be defrayed out of a common treasury, which shall be supplied by the several States in proportion to the value of all land within each State, granted or surveyed for any person, as such land and the buildings and improvements thereon shall be estimated according to such mode as the United States in Congress assembled, shall from time to time direct and appoint.

The taxes for paying that proportion shall be laid and levied by the authority and direction of the legislatures of the several States within the time agreed upon by the United States in Congress assembled.

Article IX. The United States in Congress assembled, shall have the sole and exclusive right and power of determining on peace and war, except in the cases mentioned in the sixth article — of sending and receiving ambassadors — entering into treaties and alliances, provided that no treaty of commerce shall be made whereby the legislative power of the respective States shall be restrained from imposing such imposts and duties on foreigners, as their own people are subjected to, or from prohibiting the exportation or importation of any species of goods or commodities whatsoever — of establishing rules for deciding in all cases, what captures on land or water shall be legal, and in what manner prizes taken by land or naval forces in the service of the United States shall be divided or appropriated — of granting letters of marque and reprisal in times of peace — appointing courts for the trial of piracies and felonies committed on the high seas and establishing courts for receiving and determining finally appeals in all cases of captures, provided that no member of Congress shall be appointed a judge of any of the said courts.

The United States in Congress assembled shall also be the last resort on appeal in all disputes and differences now subsisting or that hereafter may arise between two or more States concerning boundary, jurisdiction or any other causes whatever; which authority shall always be exercised in the manner following. Whenever the legislative or executive authority or lawful agent of any State in controversy with another shall present a petition to Congress stating the matter in question and praying for a hearing, notice thereof shall be given by order of Congress to the legislative or executive authority of the other State in controversy, and a day assigned for the appearance of the parties by their lawful agents, who shall then be directed to appoint by joint consent, commissioners or judges to constitute a court for hearing and determining the matter in question: but if they cannot agree, Congress shall name three persons out of each of the United States, and from the list of such persons each party shall alternately strike out one, the petitioners beginning, until the number shall be reduced to thirteen; and from that number not less than seven, nor more than nine names as Congress shall direct, shall in the presence of Congress be drawn out by lot, and the persons whose names shall be so drawn or any five of them, shall be commissioners or judges, to hear and finally determine the controversy, so always as a major part of the judges who shall hear the cause shall agree in the determination: and if either party shall neglect to attend at the day appointed, without showing reasons, which Congress shall judge sufficient, or being present shall refuse to strike, the Congress shall proceed to nominate three persons out of each State, and the secretary of Congress shall strike in behalf of such party absent or refusing; and the judgement and sentence of the court to be appointed, in the manner before prescribed, shall be final and conclusive; and if any of the parties shall refuse to submit to the authority of such court, or to appear or defend their claim or cause, the court shall nevertheless proceed to pronounce sentence, or judgement, which shall in like manner be final and decisive, the judgement or sentence and other proceedings being in either case transmitted to Congress, and lodged among the acts of Congress for the security of the parties concerned: provided that every commissioner, before he sits in judgement, shall take an oath to be administered by one of the judges of the supreme or superior court of the State, where the cause shall be tried, 'well and truly to hear and determine the matter in question, according to the best of his judgement, without favor, affection or hope of reward': provided also, that no State shall be deprived of territory for the benefit of the United States.

All controversies concerning the private right of soil claimed under different grants of two or more States, whose jurisdictions as they may respect such lands, and the States which passed such grants are adjusted, the said grants or either of them being at the same time claimed to have originated antecedent to such settlement of jurisdiction, shall on the petition of either party to the Congress of the United States, be finally determined as near as may be in the same manner as is before prescribed for deciding disputes respecting territorial jurisdiction between different States.

The United States in Congress assembled shall also have the sole and exclusive right and power of regulating the alloy and value of coin struck by their own authority, or by that of the respective States — fixing the standards of weights and measures throughout the United States — regulating the trade and managing all affairs with the Indians, not members of any of the States, provided that the legislative right of any State within its own limits be not infringed or violated — establishing or regulating post offices from one State to another, throughout all the United States, and exacting such postage on the papers passing through the same as may be requisite to defray the expenses of the said office — appointing all officers of the land forces, in the service of the United States, excepting regimental officers — appointing all the officers of the naval forces, and commissioning all officers whatever in the service of the United States — making rules for the government and regulation of the said land and naval forces, and directing their operations.

The United States in Congress assembled shall have authority to appoint a committee, to sit in the recess of Congress, to be denominated 'A Committee of the States', and to consist of one delegate from each State; and to appoint such other committees and civil officers as may be necessary for managing the general affairs of the United States under their direction — to appoint one of their members to preside, provided that no person be allowed to serve in the office of president more than one year in any term of three years; to ascertain the necessary sums of money to be raised for the service of the United States, and to appropriate and apply the same for defraying the public expenses — to borrow money, or emit bills on the credit of the United States, transmitting every half-year to the respective States an account of the sums of money so borrowed or emitted — to build and equip a navy — to agree upon the number of land forces, and to make requisitions from each State for its quota, in proportion to the number of white inhabitants in such State; which requisition shall be binding, and thereupon the legislature of each State shall appoint the regimental officers, raise the men and cloath, arm and equip them in a solid- like manner, at the expense of the United States; and the officers and men so cloathed, armed and equipped shall march to the place appointed, and within the time agreed on by the United States in Congress assembled. But if the United States in Congress assembled shall, on consideration of circumstances judge proper that any State should not raise men, or should raise a smaller number of men than the quota thereof, such extra number shall be raised, officered, cloathed, armed and equipped in the same manner as the quota of each State, unless the legislature of such State shall judge that such extra number cannot be safely spread out in the same, in which case they shall raise, officer, cloath, arm and equip as many of such extra number as they judge can be safely spared. And the officers and men so cloathed, armed, and equipped, shall march to the place appointed, and within the time agreed on by the United States in Congress assembled.

The United States in Congress assembled shall never engage in a war, nor grant letters of marque or reprisal in time of peace, nor enter into any treaties or alliances, nor coin money, nor regulate the value thereof, nor ascertain the sums and expenses necessary for the defense and welfare of the United States, or any of them, nor emit bills, nor borrow money on the credit of the United States, nor appropriate money, nor agree upon the number of vessels of war, to be built or purchased, or the number of land or sea forces to be raised, nor appoint a commander in chief of the army or navy, unless nine States assent to the same: nor shall a question on any other point, except for adjourning from day to day be determined, unless by the votes of the majority of the United States in Congress assembled.

The Congress of the United States shall have power to adjourn to any time within the year, and to any place within the United States, so that no period of adjournment be for a longer duration than the space of six months, and shall publish the journal of their proceedings monthly, except such parts thereof relating to treaties, alliances or military operations, as in their judgement require secrecy; and the yeas and nays of the delegates of each State on any question shall be entered on the journal, when it is desired by any delegates of a State, or any of them, at his or their request shall be furnished with a transcript of the said journal, except such parts as are above excepted, to lay before the legislatures of the several States.

Article X. The Committee of the States, or any nine of them, shall be authorized to execute, in the recess of Congress, such of the powers of Congress as the United States in Congress assembled, by the consent of the nine States, shall from time to time think expedient to vest them with; provided that no power be delegated to the said Committee, for the exercise of which, by the Articles of Confederation, the voice of nine States in the Congress of the United States assembled be requisite.

Article XI. Canada acceding to this confederation, and adjoining in the measures of the United States, shall be admitted into, and entitled to all the advantages of this Union; but no other colony shall be admitted into the same, unless such admission be agreed to by nine States.

Article XII. All bills of credit emitted, monies borrowed, and debts contracted by, or under the authority of Congress, before the assembling of the United States, in pursuance of the present confederation, shall be deemed and considered as a charge against the United States, for payment and satisfaction whereof the said United States, and the public faith are hereby solemnly pledged.

Article XIII. Every State shall abide by the determination of the United States in Congress assembled, on all questions which by this confederation are submitted to them. And the Articles of this Confederation shall be inviolably observed by every State, and the Union shall be perpetual; nor shall any alteration at any time hereafter be made in any of them; unless such alteration be agreed to in a Congress of the United States, and be afterwards confirmed by the legislatures of every State.

And Whereas it hath pleased the Great Governor of the World to incline the hearts of the legislatures we respectively represent in Congress, to approve of, and to authorize us to ratify the said Articles of Confederation and perpetual Union. Know Ye that we the undersigned delegates, by virtue of the power and authority to us given for that purpose, do by these presents, in the name and in behalf of our respective constituents, fully and entirely ratify and confirm each and every of the said Articles of Confederation and perpetual Union, and all and singular the matters and things therein contained: And we do further solemnly plight and engage the faith of our respective constituents, that they shall abide by the determinations of the

United States in Congress assembled, on all questions, which by the said Confederation are submitted to them. And that the Articles thereof shall be inviolably observed by the States we respectively represent, and that the Union shall be perpetual.

In Witness whereof we have hereunto set our hands in Congress. Done at Philadelphia in the State of Pennsylvania the ninth day of July in the Year of our Lord One Thousand Seven Hundred and Seventy-Eight, and in the Third Year of the independence of America.

On the part and behalf of the State of New Hampshire:
Josiah Bartlett
John Wentworth Junr. August 8th 1778

On the part and behalf of The State of Massachusetts Bay:
John Hancock
Samuel Adams
Elbridge Gerry
Francis Dana
James Lovell
Samuel Holten

On the part and behalf of the State of Rhode Island and Providence Plantations:
William Ellery
Henry Marchant
John Collins

On the part and behalf of the State of Connecticut:
Roger Sherman
Samuel Huntington
Oliver Wolcott
Titus Hosmer

Andrew Adams

On the Part and Behalf of the State of New York:
James Duane
Francis Lewis
Wm Duer
Gouv Morris

On the Part and in Behalf of the State of New Jersey,
November 26, 1778.
Jno Witherspoon
Nath. Scudder

On the part and behalf of the State of Pennsylvania:
Robt Morris
Daniel Roberdeau
John Bayard Smith
William Clingan
Joseph Reed 22nd July 1778

On the part and behalf of the State of Delaware:
Tho Mckean February 12, 1779
John Dickinson May 5th 1779
Nicholas Van Dyke

On the part and behalf of the State of Maryland:
John Hanson March 1 1781
Daniel Carroll

On the Part and Behalf of the State of Virginia:
Richard Henry Lee
John Banister
Thomas Adams
Jno Harvie
Francis Lightfoot Lee

On the part and Behalf of the State of No Carolina:
John Penn July 21st 1778

Corns Harnett
Jno Williams

On the part and behalf of the State of South Carolina:
Henry Laurens
William Henry Drayton
Jno Mathews
Richd Hutson
Thos Heyward Junr

On the part and behalf of the State of Georgia:
Jno Walton 24th July 1778
Edwd Telfair
Edwd Langworthy

# APPENDIX 4

## The Constitution of the United States

Preamble

17 september 1787

We the People of the United States, in Order to form a more perfect Union, establish Justice, insure domestic Tranquility, provide for the common defence, promote the general Welfare, and secure the Blessings of Liberty to ourselves and our Posterity, do ordain and establish this Constitution for the United States of America.

Article 1.

Section 1
All legislative Powers herein granted shall be vested in a Congress of the United States, which shall consist of a Senate and House of Representatives.

Section 2
The House of Representatives shall be composed of Members chosen every second Year by the People of the several States, and the Electors in each State shall have the Qualifications requisite for Electors of the most numerous Branch of the State Legislature.

No Person shall be a Representative who shall not have attained to the Age of twenty five Years, and been seven Years a Citizen of the United States, and who shall not, when elected, be an Inhabitant of that State in which he shall be chosen.

Representatives and direct Taxes shall be apportioned among the several States which may be included within this Union, according to their respective Numbers, which shall be determined by adding to the whole Number of free Persons, including those bound to Service for a Term of Years, and excluding Indians not taxed, three fifths of all other Persons.

The actual Enumeration shall be made within three Years after the first Meeting of the Congress of the United States, and within every subsequent Term of ten Years, in such Manner as they shall by Law direct. The Number of Representatives shall not exceed one for every thirty Thousand, but each State shall have at Least one Representative; and until such enumeration shall be made, the State of New Hampshire shall be entitled to choose three, Massachusetts eight, Rhode Island and Providence Plantations one, Connecticut five, New York six, New Jersey four, Pennsylvania eight, Delaware one, Maryland six, Virginia ten, North Carolina five, South Carolina five and Georgia three.

When vacancies happen in the Representation

from any State, the Executive Authority thereof shall issue Writs of Election to fill such Vacancies.

The House of Representatives shall choose their Speaker and other Officers; and shall have the sole Power of Impeachment.

Section 3
The Senate of the United States shall be composed of two Senators from each State, chosen by the Legislature thereof, for six Years; and each Senator shall have one Vote.

Immediately after they shall be assembled in Consequence of the first Election, they shall be divided as equally as may be into three Classes. The Seats of the Senators of the first Class shall be vacated at the Expiration of the second Year, of the second Class at the Expiration of the fourth Year, and of the third Class at the Expiration of the sixth Year, so that one third may be chosen every second Year; and if Vacancies happen by Resignation, or otherwise, during the Recess of the Legislature of any State, the Executive thereof may make temporary Appointments until the next Meeting of the Legislature, which shall then fill such Vacancies.

No person shall be a Senator who shall not have attained to the Age of thirty Years, and been nine Years a Citizen of the United

States, and who shall not, when elected, be an Inhabitant of that State for which he shall be chosen.

The Vice President of the United States shall be President of the Senate, but shall have no Vote, unless they be equally divided.

The Senate shall choose their other Officers, and also a President pro tempore, in the absence of the Vice President, or when he shall exercise the Office of President of the United States.

The Senate shall have the sole Power to try all Impeachments. When sitting for that Purpose, they shall be on Oath or Affirmation. When the President of the United States is tried, the Chief Justice shall preside: And no Person shall be convicted without the Concurrence of two thirds of the Members present.

Judgment in Cases of Impeachment shall not extend further than to removal from Office, and disqualification to hold and enjoy any Office of honor, Trust or Profit under the United States: but the Party convicted shall nevertheless be liable and subject to Indictment, Trial, Judgment and Punishment, according to Law.

Section 4
The Times, Places and Manner of holding

Elections for Senators and Representatives, shall be prescribed in each State by the Legislature thereof; but the Congress may at any time by Law make or alter such Regulations, except as to the Place of Choosing Senators.

The Congress shall assemble at least once in every Year, and such Meeting shall be on the first Monday in December, unless they shall by Law appoint a different Day.

Section 5
Each House shall be the Judge of the Elections, Returns and Qualifications of its own Members, and a Majority of each shall constitute a Quorum to do Business; but a smaller number may adjourn from day to day, and may be authorized to compel the Attendance of absent Members, in such Manner, and under such Penalties as each House may provide.

Each House may determine the Rules of its Proceedings, punish its Members for disorderly Behavior, and, with the Concurrence of two-thirds, expel a Member.

Each House shall keep a Journal of its Proceedings, and from time to time publish the same, excepting such Parts as may in their Judgment require Secrecy; and the Yeas and Nays of the Members of either House on any question shall, at the Desire of one fifth of those Present, be entered on the Journal.

Neither House, during the Session of Congress, shall, without the Consent of the other, adjourn for more than three days, nor to any other Place than that in which the two Houses shall be sitting.

Section 6
The Senators and Representatives shall receive a Compensation for their Services, to be ascertained by Law, and paid out of the Treasury of the United States. They shall in all Cases, except Treason, Felony and Breach of the Peace, be privileged from Arrest during their Attendance at the Session of their respective Houses, and in going to and returning from the same; and for any Speech or Debate in either House, they shall not be questioned in any other Place.

No Senator or Representative shall, during the Time for which he was elected, be appointed to any civil Office under the Authority of the United States which shall have been created, or the Emoluments whereof shall have been increased during such time; and no Person holding any Office under the United States, shall be a Member of either House during his Continuance in Office.

Section 7
All bills for raising Revenue shall

originate in the House of Representatives; but the Senate may propose or concur with Amendments as on other Bills.

Every Bill which shall have passed the House of Representatives and the Senate, shall, before it become a Law, be presented to the President of the United States; If he approve he shall sign it, but if not he shall return it, with his Objections to that House in which it shall have originated, who shall enter the Objections at large on their Journal, and proceed to reconsider it. If after such Reconsideration two thirds of that House shall agree to pass the Bill, it shall be sent, together with the Objections, to the other House, by which it shall likewise be reconsidered, and if approved by two thirds of that House, it shall become a Law. But in all such Cases the Votes of both Houses shall be determined by Yeas and Nays, and the Names of the Persons voting for and against the Bill shall be entered on the Journal of each House respectively. If any Bill shall not be returned by the President within ten Days (Sundays excepted) after it shall have been presented to him, the Same shall be a Law, in like Manner as if he had signed it, unless the Congress by their Adjournment prevent its Return, in which Case it shall not be a Law.

Every Order, Resolution, or Vote to which the Concurrence of the Senate and House of

Representatives may be necessary (except on a question of Adjournment) shall be presented to the President of the United States; and before the Same shall take Effect, shall be approved by him, or being disapproved by him, shall be repassed by two thirds of the Senate and House of Representatives, according to the Rules and Limitations prescribed in the Case of a Bill.

Section 8
The Congress shall have Power To lay and collect Taxes, Duties, Imposts and Excises, to pay the Debts and provide for the common Defence and general Welfare of the United States; but all Duties, Imposts and Excises shall be uniform throughout the United States;

To borrow money on the credit of the United States;

To regulate Commerce with foreign Nations, and among the several States, and with the Indian Tribes;

To establish an uniform Rule of Naturalization, and uniform Laws on the subject of Bankruptcies throughout the United States;

To coin Money, regulate the Value thereof, and of foreign Coin, and fix the Standard of Weights and Measures;

To provide for the Punishment of counterfeiting the Securities and current Coin of the United States;

To establish Post Offices and Post Roads;

To promote the Progress of Science and useful Arts, by securing for limited Times to Authors and Inventors the exclusive Right to their respective Writings and Discoveries;

To constitute Tribunals inferior to the supreme Court;

To define and punish Piracies and Felonies committed on the high Seas, and Offenses against the Law of Nations;

To declare War, grant Letters of Marque and Reprisal, and make Rules concerning Captures on Land and Water;

To raise and support Armies, but no Appropriation of Money to that Use shall be for a longer Term than two Years;

To provide and maintain a Navy;

To make Rules for the Government and Regulation of the land and naval Forces;

To provide for calling forth the Militia

to execute the Laws of the Union, suppress Insurrections and repel Invasions;

To provide for organizing, arming, and disciplining the Militia, and for governing such Part of them as may be employed in the Service of the United States, reserving to the States respectively, the Appointment of the Officers, and the Authority of training the Militia according to the discipline prescribed by Congress;

To exercise exclusive Legislation in all Cases whatsoever, over such District (not exceeding ten Miles square) as may, by Cession of particular States, and the acceptance of Congress, become the Seat of the Government of the United States, and to exercise like Authority over all Places purchased by the Consent of the Legislature of the State in which the Same shall be, for the Erection of Forts, Magazines, Arsenals, dock-Yards, and other needful Buildings; And

To make all Laws which shall be necessary and proper for carrying into Execution the foregoing Powers, and all other Powers vested by this Constitution in the Government of the United States, or in any Department or Officer thereof.

Section 9
The Migration or Importation of such Persons as any of the States now existing

shall think proper to admit, shall not be prohibited by the Congress prior to the Year one thousand eight hundred and eight, but a tax or duty may be imposed on such Importation, not exceeding ten dollars for each Person.

The privilege of the Writ of Habeas Corpus shall not be suspended, unless when in Cases of Rebellion or Invasion the public Safety may require it.

No Bill of Attainder or ex post facto Law shall be passed.

No capitation, or other direct, Tax shall be laid, unless in Proportion to the Census or Enumeration herein before directed to be taken.

No Tax or Duty shall be laid on Articles exported from any State.

No Preference shall be given by any Regulation of Commerce or Revenue to the Ports of one State over those of another: nor shall Vessels bound to, or from, one State, be obliged to enter, clear, or pay Duties in another.

No Money shall be drawn from the Treasury, but in Consequence of Appropriations made by Law; and a regular Statement and Account of the Receipts and Expenditures of all public Money shall be published from time to time.

No Title of Nobility shall be granted by the United States: And no Person holding any Office of Profit or Trust under them, shall, without the Consent of the Congress, accept of any present, Emolument, Office, or Title, of any kind whatever, from any King, Prince or foreign State.

Section 10
No State shall enter into any Treaty, Alliance, or Confederation; grant Letters of Marque and Reprisal; coin Money; emit Bills of Credit; make any Thing but gold and silver Coin a Tender in Payment of Debts; pass any Bill of Attainder, ex post facto Law, or Law impairing the Obligation of Contracts, or grant any Title of Nobility.

No State shall, without the Consent of the Congress, lay any Imposts or Duties on Imports or Exports, except what may be absolutely necessary for executing its inspection Laws: and the net Produce of all Duties and Imposts, laid by any State on Imports or Exports, shall be for the Use of the Treasury of the United States; and all such Laws shall be subject to the Revision and Control of the Congress.

No State shall, without the Consent of Congress, lay any duty of Tonnage, keep Troops, or Ships of War in time of Peace, enter into any Agreement or Compact with another State, or with a foreign Power, or engage in War, unless actually invaded, or in such imminent Danger as will not admit of delay.

Article 2.

Section 1
The executive Power shall be vested in a President of the United States of America. He shall hold his Office during the Term of four Years, and, together with the Vice-President chosen for the same Term, be elected, as follows:

Each State shall appoint, in such Manner as the Legislature thereof may direct, a Number of Electors, equal to the whole Number of Senators and Representatives to which the State may be entitled in the Congress: but no Senator or Representative, or Person holding an Office of Trust or Profit under the United States, shall be appointed an Elector.

The Electors shall meet in their respective States, and vote by Ballot for two persons, of whom one at least shall not lie an Inhabitant of the same State with themselves. And they shall make a List of all the Persons voted for, and of the Number of Votes for each; which List they shall sign and certify, and transmit sealed to the Seat of the Government of the United States, directed to the President of the

Senate. The President of the Senate shall, in the Presence
of the Senate and House of Representatives, open all the Certificates,. and the Votes shall then be counted. The Person having the greatest Number of Votes shall be the President, if such Number be a Majority of the whole Number of Electors appointed; and if there be more than one who have such Majority, and have an equal Number of Votes, then the House of Representatives shall immediately choose by Ballot one of them for President; and if no Person have a Majority, then from the five highest on the List the said House shall in like Manner choose the President. But in choosing the President, the Votes shall be taken by States, the Representation from each State having one Vote; a quorum for this Purpose shall consist of a Member or Members from two-thirds of the States, and a Majority of all the States shall be necessary to a Choice. In every Case, after the Choice of the President, the Person having the greatest Number of Votes of the Electors shall be the Vice President. But if there should remain two or more who have equal Votes, the Senate shall choose from them by Ballot the Vice-President.

The Congress may determine the Time of choosing the Electors, and the Day on which they shall give their Votes; which Day shall be the same throughout the United States.

No person except a natural born Citizen, or a Citizen of the United States, at the time of the Adoption of this Constitution, shall be eligible to the Office of President; neither shall any Person be eligible to that Office who shall not have attained to the Age of thirty-five Years, and been fourteen Years a Resident within the United States.

In Case of the Removal of the President from Office, or of his Death, Resignation, or Inability to discharge the Powers and Duties of the said Office, the same shall devolve on the Vice President, and the Congress may by Law provide for the Case of Removal, Death, Resignation or Inability, both of the President and Vice President, declaring what Officer shall then act as President, and such Officer shall act accordingly, until the Disability be removed, or a President shall be elected.

The President shall, at stated Times, receive for his Services, a Compensation, which shall neither be increased nor diminished during the Period for which he shall have been elected, and he shall not receive within that Period any other Emolument from the United States, or any of them.

Before he enter on the Execution of his Office, he shall take the following Oath or Affirmation:

"I do solemnly swear (or affirm) that I will faithfully execute the Office of President of the United States, and will to the best of my Ability, preserve, protect and defend the Constitution of the United States."

Section 2
The President shall be Commander in Chief of the Army and Navy of the United States, and of the Militia of the several States, when called into the actual Service of the United States; he may require the Opinion, in writing, of the principal Officer in each of the executive Departments, upon any subject relating to the Duties of their respective Offices, and he shall have Power to Grant Reprieves and Pardons for Offenses against the United States, except in Cases of Impeachment.

He shall have Power, by and with the Advice and Consent of the Senate, to make Treaties, provided two thirds of the Senators present concur; and he shall nominate, and by and with the Advice and Consent of the Senate, shall appoint Ambassadors, other public Ministers and Consuls, Judges of the supreme Court, and all other Officers of the United States, whose Appointments are not herein otherwise provided for, and which shall be established by Law: but the Congress may by Law vest the Appointment of such inferior Officers, as they think proper, in the President alone, in the Courts of Law, or in the Heads of Departments.

The President shall have Power to fill up all Vacancies that may happen during the Recess of the Senate, by granting Commissions which shall expire at the End of their next Session.

Section 3
He shall from time to time give to the Congress Information of the State of the Union, and recommend to their Consideration such Measures as he shall judge necessary and expedient; he may, on extraordinary Occasions, convene both Houses, or either of them, and in Case of Disagreement between them, with Respect to the Time of Adjournment, he may adjourn them to such Time as he shall think proper; he shall receive Ambassadors and other public Ministers; he shall take Care that the Laws be faithfully executed, and shall Commission all the Officers of the United States.

Section 4
The President, Vice President and all civil Officers of the United States, shall be removed from Office on Impeachment for, and Conviction of, Treason, Bribery, or other high Crimes and Misdemeanors.

Article 3.

Section 1
The judicial Power of the United States, shall be vested in one supreme Court, and in such inferior Courts as the Congress may from time to time ordain and establish. The Judges, both of the supreme and inferior Courts, shall hold their Offices during good Behavior, and shall, at stated Times, receive for their Services a Compensation which shall not be diminished during their Continuance in Office.

Section 2
The judicial Power shall extend to all Cases, in Law and Equity, arising under this Constitution, the Laws of the United States, and Treaties made, or which shall be made, under their Authority; to all Cases affecting Ambassadors, other public Ministers and Consuls; to all Cases of admiralty and maritime Jurisdiction; to Controversies to which the United States shall be a Party; to Controversies between two or more States; between a State and Citizens of another State; between Citizens of different States; between Citizens of the same State claiming Lands under Grants of different States, and between a State, or the Citizens thereof, and foreign States, Citizens or Subjects.

In all Cases affecting Ambassadors, other public Ministers and Consuls, and those in which a State shall be Party, the supreme Court shall have original Jurisdiction. In all the other Cases before mentioned, the supreme Court shall have appellate Jurisdiction, both as to Law and Fact, with such Exceptions, and under such Regulations as the Congress shall make.

The Trial of all Crimes, except in Cases of Impeachment, shall be by Jury; and such Trial shall be held in the State where the said Crimes shall have been committed; but when not committed within any State, the Trial shall be at such Place or Places as the Congress may by Law have directed.

Section 3
Treason against the United States, shall consist only in levying War against them, or in adhering to their Enemies, giving them Aid and Comfort. No Person shall be convicted of Treason unless on the Testimony of two Witnesses to the same overt Act, or on Confession in open Court.

The Congress shall have power to declare the Punishment of Treason, but no Attainder of Treason shall work Corruption of Blood, or Forfeiture except during the Life of the Person attainted.

Article 4.

## Section 1

Full Faith and Credit shall be given in each State to the public Acts, Records, and judicial Proceedings of every other State. And the Congress may by general Laws prescribe the Manner in which such Acts, Records and Proceedings shall be proved, and the Effect thereof.

## Section 2

The Citizens of each State shall be entitled to all Privileges and Immunities of Citizens in the several States.

A Person charged in any State with Treason, Felony, or other Crime, who shall flee from Justice, and be found in another State, shall on demand of the executive Authority of the State from which he fled, be delivered up, to be removed to the State having Jurisdiction of the Crime.

No Person held to Service or Labour in one State, under the Laws thereof, escaping into another, shall, in Consequence of any Law or Regulation therein, be discharged from such Service or Labour, But shall be delivered up on Claim of the Party to whom such Service or Labour may be due.

## Section 3

New States may be admitted by the Congress

into this Union; but no new States shall be formed or erected within the Jurisdiction of any other State; nor any State be formed by the Junction of two or more States, or parts of States, without the Consent of the Legislatures of the States concerned as well as of the Congress.

The Congress shall have Power to dispose of and make all needful Rules and Regulations respecting the Territory or other Property belonging to the United States; and nothing in this Constitution shall be so construed as to Prejudice any Claims of the United States, or of any particular State.

Section 4
The United States shall guarantee to every State in this Union a Republican Form of Government, and shall protect each of them against Invasion; and on Application of the Legislature, or of the Executive (when the Legislature cannot be convened) against domestic Violence.

Article 5.

The Congress, whenever two thirds of both Houses shall deem it necessary, shall propose Amendments to this Constitution, or, on the Application of the Legislatures of two thirds of the several States, shall call a Convention for proposing Amendments, which, in either Case, shall be valid to all Intents and Purposes, as part of

this Constitution, when ratified by the Legislatures of three fourths of the several States, or by Conventions in three fourths thereof, as the one or the other Mode of Ratification may be proposed by the Congress; Provided that no Amendment which may be made prior to the Year One
thousand eight hundred and eight shall in any Manner affect the first and fourth Clauses in the Ninth Section of the first Article; and that no State, without its Consent, shall be deprived of its equal Suffrage in the Senate.

Article 6.

All Debts contracted and Engagements entered into, before the Adoption of this Constitution, shall be as valid against the United States under this Constitution, as under the Confederation.

This Constitution, and the Laws of the United States which shall be made in Pursuance thereof; and all Treaties made, or which shall be made, under the Authority of the United States, shall be the supreme Law of the Land; and the Judges in every State shall be bound thereby, any Thing in the Constitution or Laws of any State to the Contrary notwithstanding.

The Senators and Representatives before

mentioned, and the Members of the several State Legislatures, and all executive and judicial Officers, both of the United States and of the several States, shall be bound by Oath or Affirmation, to support this Constitution; but no religious Test shall ever be required as a Qualification to any Office or public Trust under the United States.

Article 7.

The Ratification of the Conventions of nine States, shall be sufficient for the Establishment of this Constitution between the States so ratifying the Same.

Done in Convention by the Unanimous Consent of the States present the Seventeenth Day of September in the Year of our Lord one thousand seven hundred and Eighty seven and of the Independence of the United States of America the Twelfth. In Witness whereof We have hereunto subscribed our Names.

George Washington - President and deputy from Virginia

New Hampshire - John Langdon, Nicholas Gilman

Massachusetts - Nathaniel Gorham, Rufus King

Connecticut - William Samuel Johnson, Roger Sherman

New York - Alexander Hamilton

New Jersey - William Livingston, David Brearley, William

Paterson, Jonathan Dayton

Pennsylvania - Benjamin Franklin, Thomas Mifflin, Robert Morris, George Clymer, Thomas Fitzsimons, Jared Ingersoll, James Wilson, Gouvernour Morris

Delaware - George Read, Gunning Bedford Jr., John Dickinson, Richard Bassett, Jacob Broom

Maryland - James McHenry, Daniel of St Thomas Jenifer, Daniel Carroll

Virginia - John Blair, James Madison Jr.

North Carolina - William Blount, Richard Dobbs Spaight, Hugh Williamson

South Carolina - John Rutledge, Charles Cotesworth Pinckney, Charles Pinckney, Pierce Butler

Georgia - William Few, Abraham Baldwin

Attest: William Jackson, Secretary

# APPENDIX 5

## Bill of Rights

Amendment 1
Congress shall make no law respecting an establishment of religion, or prohibiting the free exercise thereof; or abridging the freedom of speech, or of the press; or the right of the people peaceably to assemble, and to petition the Government for a redress of grievances.

Amendment 2
A well regulated Militia, being necessary to the security of a free State, the right of the people to keep and bear Arms, shall not be infringed.

Amendment 3
No Soldier shall, in time of peace be quartered in any house, without the consent of the Owner, nor in time of war, but in a manner to be prescribed by law.

Amendment 4
The right of the people to be secure in their persons, houses, papers, and effects, against unreasonable searches and seizures, shall not be violated, and no Warrants shall issue, but upon probable cause, supported by Oath or affirmation, and particularly describing the place to be searched, and the persons or things to be seized.

## Amendment 5

No person shall be held to answer for a capital, or otherwise infamous crime, unless on a presentment or indictment of a Grand Jury, except in cases arising in the land or naval forces, or in the Militia, when in actual service in time of War or public danger; nor shall any person be subject for the same offense to be twice put in jeopardy of life or limb; nor shall be compelled in any criminal case to be a witness against himself, nor be deprived of life, liberty, or property, without due process of law; nor shall private property be taken for public use, without just compensation.

## Amendment 6

In all criminal prosecutions, the accused shall enjoy the right to a speedy and public trial, by an impartial jury of the State and district wherein the crime shall have been committed, which district shall have been previously ascertained by law, and to be informed of the nature and cause of the accusation; to be confronted with the witnesses against him; to have compulsory process for obtaining witnesses in his favor, and to have the Assistance of Counsel for his defence.

## Amendment 7

In Suits at common law, where the value in controversy shall exceed twenty dollars, the right of trial by jury shall be preserved, and no fact tried by a jury, shall be otherwise re-examined in any Court of the United States, than according to the rules of the common law.

Amendment 8
Excessive bail shall not be required, nor excessive fines imposed, nor cruel and unusual punishments inflicted.

Amendment 9
The enumeration in the Constitution, of certain rights, shall not be construed to deny or disparage others retained by the people.

Amendment 10
The powers not delegated to the United States by the Constitution, nor prohibited by it to the States, are reserved to the States respectively, or to the people.

*Secure the Blessings of Liberty*

# APPENDIX 6

## Amendments Following The Bill of Rights

Amendment 11    (1794)
The Judicial power of the United States shall not be construed to extend to any suit in law or equity, commenced or prosecuted against one of the United States by Citizens of another State, or by Citizens or Subjects of any Foreign State.

Amendment 12 (1803)
The Electors shall meet in their respective states, and vote by ballot for President and Vice-President, one of whom, at least, shall not be an inhabitant of the same state with themselves; they shall name in their ballots the person voted for as President, and in distinct ballots the person voted for as Vice-President, and they shall make distinct lists of all persons voted for as President, and of all persons voted for as Vice-President and of the number of votes for each, which lists they shall sign and certify, and transmit sealed to the seat of the government of the United States, directed to the President of the Senate;

The President of the Senate shall, in the presence of the Senate and House of Representatives, open all the certificates and the votes shall then be counted;

The person having the greatest Number of votes for President, shall be the President, if such number be a majority of the whole number of Electors appointed; and if no person have such majority, then from the persons having the highest numbers not exceeding three on the list of those voted for as President, the House of Representatives shall choose immediately, by ballot, the President. But in choosing the President, the votes shall be taken by states, the representation from each state having one vote; a quorum for this purpose shall consist of a member or members from two-thirds of the states, and a majority of all the states shall be necessary to a choice. And if the House of Representatives shall not choose a President whenever the right of choice shall devolve upon them, before the fourth day of March next following, then the Vice-President shall act as President, as in the case of the death or other constitutional disability of the President.

The person having the greatest number of votes as Vice-President, shall be the Vice-President, if such number be a majority of the whole number of Electors appointed, and if no person have a majority, then from the two highest numbers on the list, the Senate shall choose the Vice-President; a quorum for the purpose shall consist of two-thirds of the whole number of Senators, and a majority of the whole number shall be necessary to a choice. But no person constitutionally ineligible to the office of President shall be eligible to that of Vice-President of the United States.

Amendment 13 (1865)
1. Neither slavery nor involuntary servitude, except as a punishment for crime whereof the party shall have been duly convicted, shall exist within the United States, or any place subject to their jurisdiction.

2. Congress shall have power to enforce this article by appropriate legislation.

Amendment 14 (1866)
1. All persons born or naturalized in the United States, and subject to the jurisdiction thereof, are citizens of the United States and of the State wherein they reside. No State shall make or enforce any law which shall abridge the privileges or immunities of citizens of the United States; nor shall any State deprive any person of life, liberty, or property, without due process of law; nor deny to any person within its jurisdiction the equal protection of the laws.

2. Representatives shall be apportioned among the several States according to

their respective numbers, counting the whole number of persons in each State, excluding Indians not taxed. But when the right to vote at any election for the choice of electors for President and Vice-President of the United States, Representatives in Congress, the Executive and Judicial officers of a State, or the members of the Legislature thereof, is denied to any of the male inhabitants of such State, being twenty-one years of age, and citizens of the United States, or in any way abridged, except for participation in rebellion, or other crime, the basis of representation therein shall be reduced in the proportion which the number of such male citizens shall bear to the whole number of male citizens twenty-one years of age in such State.

3. No person shall be a Senator or Representative in Congress, or elector of President and Vice-President, or hold any office, civil or military, under the United States, or under any State, who, having previously taken an oath, as a member of Congress, or as an officer of the United States, or as a member of any State legislature, or as an executive or judicial officer of any State, to support the Constitution of the United States, shall have engaged in insurrection or rebellion against the same, or given aid or comfort to the enemies thereof. But

Congress may by a vote of two-thirds of each House, remove such disability.

4. The validity of the public debt of the United States, authorized by law, including debts incurred for payment of pensions and bounties for services in suppressing insurrection or rebellion, shall not be questioned. But neither the United States nor any State shall assume or pay any debt or obligation incurred in aid of insurrection or rebellion against the United States, or any claim for the loss or emancipation of any slave; but all such debts, obligations and claims shall be held illegal and void.

5. The Congress shall have power to enforce, by appropriate legislation, the provisions of this article.

Amendment 15 (1869)
1. The right of citizens of the United States to vote shall not be denied or abridged by the United States or by any State on account of race, color, or previous condition of servitude.

2. The Congress shall have power to enforce this article by appropriate legislation.

Amendment 16 (1909)
The Congress shall have power to lay and collect taxes on incomes, from whatever source derived, without apportionment among

the several States, and without regard to any census or enumeration.

Amendment 17 (1912)
The Senate of the United States shall be composed of two Senators from each State, elected by the people thereof, for six years; and each Senator shall have one vote. The electors in each State shall have the qualifications requisite for electors of the most numerous branch of the State legislatures.

When vacancies happen in the representation of any State in the Senate, the executive authority of such State shall issue writs of election to fill such vacancies: Provided, That the legislature of any State may empower the executive thereof to make temporary appointments until the people fill the vacancies by election as the legislature may direct.

This amendment shall not be so construed as to affect the election or term of any Senator chosen before it becomes valid as part of the Constitution.

Amendment 18 (1917)
1. After one year from the ratification of this article the manufacture, sale, or transportation of intoxicating liquors within, the importation thereof into, or the exportation thereof from the United States and all territory subject to the

jurisdiction thereof for beverage purposes is hereby prohibited.

2. The Congress and the several States shall have concurrent power to enforce this article by appropriate legislation.

3. This article shall be inoperative unless it shall have been ratified as an amendment to the Constitution by the legislatures of the several States, as provided in the Constitution, within seven years from the date of the submission hereof to the States by the Congress.

Amendment 19 (1919)
The right of citizens of the United States to vote shall not be denied or abridged by the United States or by any State on account of sex.

Congress shall have power to enforce this article by appropriate legislation.

Amendment 20 (1932)
1. The terms of the President and Vice President shall end at noon on the 20th day of January, and the terms of Senators and Representatives at noon on the 3d day of January, of the years in which such terms would have ended if this article had not been ratified; and the terms of their successors shall then begin.

2. The Congress shall assemble at least

once in every year, and such meeting shall begin at noon on the 3d day of January, unless they shall by law appoint a different day.

3. If, at the time fixed for the beginning of the term of the President, the President elect shall have died, the Vice President elect shall become President. If a President shall not have been chosen before the time fixed for the beginning of his term, or if the President elect shall have failed to qualify, then the Vice President elect shall act as President until a President shall have qualified; and the Congress may by law provide for the case wherein neither a President elect nor a Vice President elect shall have qualified, declaring who shall then act as President, or the manner in which one who is to act shall be selected, and such person shall act accordingly until a President or Vice President shall have qualified.

4. The Congress may by law provide for the case of the death of any of the persons from whom the House of Representatives may choose a President whenever the right of choice shall have devolved upon them, and for the case of the death of any of the persons from whom the Senate may choose a Vice President whenever the right of choice shall have devolved upon them.

5. Sections 1 and 2 shall take effect on

the 15th day of October following the ratification of this article.

6. This article shall be inoperative unless it shall have been ratified as an amendment to the Constitution by the legislatures of three-fourths of the several States within seven years from the date of its submission.

Amendment 21 (1933)
1. The eighteenth article of amendment to the Constitution of the United States is hereby repealed.

2. The transportation or importation into any State, Territory, or possession of the United States for delivery or use therein of intoxicating liquors, in violation of the laws thereof, is hereby prohibited.

3. The article shall be inoperative unless it shall have been ratified as an amendment to the Constitution by conventions in the several States, as provided in the Constitution, within seven years from the date of the submission hereof to the States by the Congress.

Amendment 22 (1947)
1. No person shall be elected to the office of the President more than twice, and no person who has held the office of President, or acted as President, for

more than two years of a term to which some other person was elected President shall be elected to the office of the President more than once. But this Article shall not apply to any person holding the office of President, when this Article was proposed by the Congress, and shall not prevent any person who may be holding the office of President, or acting as President, during the term within which this Article becomes operative from holding the office of President or acting as President during the remainder of such term.

2. This article shall be inoperative unless it shall have been ratified as an amendment to the Constitution by the legislatures of three-fourths of the several States within seven years from the date of its submission to the States by the Congress.

Amendment 23 (1960)
1. The District constituting the seat of Government of the United States shall appoint in such manner as the Congress may direct: A number of electors of President and Vice President equal to the whole number of Senators and Representatives in Congress to which the District would be entitled if it were a State, but in no event more than the least populous State; they shall be in addition to those appointed by the States, but they shall be considered, for the purposes of the election of President and Vice President,

to be electors appointed by a State; and they shall meet in the District and perform such duties as provided by the twelfth article of amendment.

2. The Congress shall have power to enforce this article by appropriate legislation.

Amendment 24 (1962)
1. The right of citizens of the United States to vote in any primary or other election for President or Vice President, for electors for President or Vice President, or for Senator or Representative in Congress, shall not be denied or abridged by the United States or any State by reason of failure to pay any poll tax or other tax.

2. The Congress shall have power to enforce this article by appropriate legislation.

Amendment 25 (1965)
1. In case of the removal of the President from office or of his death or resignation, the Vice President shall become President.

2. Whenever there is a vacancy in the office of the Vice President, the President shall nominate a Vice President who shall take office upon confirmation by a majority vote of both Houses of Congress.

3. Whenever the President transmits to the President pro tempore of the Senate and the Speaker of the House of Representatives his written declaration that he is unable to discharge the powers and duties of his office, and until he transmits to them a written declaration to the contrary, such powers and duties shall be discharged by the Vice President as Acting President.

4. Whenever the Vice President and a majority of either the principal officers of the executive departments or of such other body as Congress may by law provide, transmit to the President pro tempore of the Senate and the Speaker of the House of Representatives their written declaration that the President is unable to discharge the powers and duties of his office, the Vice President shall immediately assume the powers and duties of the office as Acting President.

Thereafter, when the President transmits to the President pro tempore of the Senate and the Speaker of the House of Representatives his written declaration that no inability exists, he shall resume the powers and duties of his office unless the Vice President and a majority of either the principal officers of the executive department or of such other body as Congress may by law provide, transmit within four days to the President pro tempore of the Senate and the Speaker of the House of Representatives their written declaration that the President is unable to discharge the powers and duties of his office. Thereupon Congress shall decide the issue, assembling within forty eight hours for that purpose if not in session. If the Congress, within twenty one days after receipt of the latter written declaration, or, if Congress is not in session, within twenty one days after Congress is required to assemble, determines by two thirds vote of both Houses that the President is unable to discharge the powers and duties of his office, the Vice President shall continue to discharge the same as Acting President; otherwise, the President shall resume the powersand duties of his office.

Amendment 26 (1971)
1. The right of citizens of the United States, who are eighteen years of age or older, to vote shall not be denied or abridged by the United States or by any State on account of age.

2. The Congress shall have power to enforce this article by appropriate legislation.

Amendment 27 (1992)
No law, varying the compensation for the services of the Senators and Representatives, shall take effect, until an election of Representatives shall have intervened.